Richard Dormer

Drum Belly

Methuen Dra

Bloomsbury Methuen Drama

An imprint of Bloomsbury Publishing Plc

50 Bedford Square   175 Fifth Avenue
London   New York
WC1B 3DP   NY 10010
UK   USA

www.bloomsbury.com

First published 2013

British Library Cataloguing-in-Publication Data
A catalogue record for this book is available from the British Library

ISBN
PB: 978-1-4725-1373-1
ePub: 978-1-4725-0877-5
ePDF: 978-1-4725-1375-5

Typeset by Country Setting, Kingsdown, Kent CT14 8ES
Printed and bound in Great Britain

WORLD PREMIERE
AN ABBEY THEATRE COMMISSION

ABBEY THEATRE

DRUM BELLY

RICHARD DORMER

Honour your blood. Be true to it.

The Abbey Theatre gratefully acknowledges
the financial support of the Arts Council of
Ireland and the support of the Department
of the Arts, Heritage and the Gaeltacht.

ABBEY THEATRE AMHARCLANN NA MAINISTREACH

THE ABBEY THEATRE is Ireland's national theatre. It was founded by W.B. Yeats and Lady Augusta Gregory. Since it first opened its doors in 1904 the theatre has played a vital and often controversial role in the literary, social and cultural life of Ireland.

In 1911 the Abbey Theatre first toured internationally and continues to be an ambassador for Irish arts and culture worldwide.

The Abbey produces an annual programme of diverse, engaging, innovative Irish and international theatre and invests in and promotes new Irish writers and artists.

We do this by placing the writer and theatre-maker at the heart of all that we do, commissioning and producing exciting new work and creating discourse and debate on the political, cultural and social issues of the day. Our aim is to present great theatre art in a national context so that the stories told on stage have a resonance with artists and audiences alike.

Over the years, the Abbey Theatre has nurtured and premiered the work of major playwrights such as J.M. Synge and Sean O'Casey as well as contemporary classics from the likes of Sebastian Barry, Marina Carr, Bernard Farrell, Brian Friel, Frank McGuinness, Thomas Kilroy, Tom MacIntyre, Tom Murphy, Mark O'Rowe, Billy Roche and Sam Shepard. We also support a new generation of Irish writers at the Abbey Theatre including Gary Duggan, Stacey Gregg, Nancy Harris, Elaine Murphy and Carmel Winters.

None of this can happen without our audiences and our supporters. Annie Horniman provided crucial financial support to the Abbey in its first years. Many others have followed her lead by investing in and supporting our work.

IS Í AMHARCLANN NA MAINISTREACH amharclann náisiúnta na hÉireann. W.B. Yeats agus an Bantiarna Augusta Gregory a bhunaigh í. Riamh anall ón uair a osclaíodh a doirse i 1904, ghlac an amharclann ról an-tábhachtach agus, go minic, ról a bhí sách conspóideach, i saol liteartha, sóisialta agus cultúrtha na hÉireann.

I 1911 is ea a chuaigh complacht Amharclann na Mainistreach ar camchuairt idirnáisiúnta den chéad uair agus leanann sí i gcónaí de bheith ina hambasadóir ar fud an domhain d'ealaíona agus cultúr na hÉireann.

Léiríonn Amharclann na Mainistreach clár amharclannaíochta Éireannach agus idirnáisiúnta in aghaidh na bliana atá ilghnéitheach, tarraingteach agus nuálach agus agus infheistíonn sí a cuid acmhainní i scríbhneoirí agus ealaíontóirí nua de chuid na hÉireann agus cuireann sí chun cinn iad.

Déanaimid é sin tríd an scríbhneoir agus an t-amharclannóir a chur i gcroílár an uile ní a dhéanaimid, trí shaothar nua spreagúil a choimisiúnú agus a léiriú agus trí dhioscúrsa agus díospóireacht a chruthú i dtaobh cheisteanna polaitiúla, cultúrtha agus sóisialta na linne. Is í an aidhm atá againn ealaín amharclannaíochta den scoth a láithriú i gcomhthéacs náisiúnta ionas go mbeidh dáimh ag lucht ealaíne agus lucht féachana araon leis na scéalta a bhíonn á n-aithris ar an stáitse.

In imeacht na mblianta, rinne Amharclann na Mainistreach saothar mórdhrámadóirí ar nós J.M. Synge agus Sean O'Casey a chothú agus a chéadléiriú, mar a rinne sí freisin i gcás clasaicí comhaimseartha ó dhrámadóirí amhail Sebastian Barry, Marina Carr, Bernard Farrell, Brian Friel, Frank McGuinness, Thomas Kilroy, Tom MacIntyre, Tom Murphy, Mark O'Rowe, Billy Roche agus Sam Shepard.

Tugaimid tacaíocht freisin don ghlúin nua Scríbhneoirí Éireannacha in Amharclann na Mainistreach, lena n-áirítear Gary Duggan, Stacey Gregg, Nancy Harris, Elaine Murphy agus Carmel Winters.

Ní féidir aon ní den chineál sin a thabhairt i gcrích gan ár lucht féachana agus ár lucht tacaíochta. Sholáthair Annie Horniman tacaíocht airgid ríthábhachtach don Mhainistir siar i mblianta tosaigh na hamharclainne. Lean iliomad daoine eile an dea-shampla ceannródaíochta sin uaithi ó shin trí infheistíocht a dhéanamh inár gcuid oibre agus tacaíocht a thabhairt dúinn.

CAST (IN ORDER OF APPEARANCE)

Harvey Marr	Liam Carney
Walter Sorrow	Gerard Byrne
Johnny 'The Fox' Rourke	Ciarán O'Brien
Willy 'Wicklow' Hill	Ronan Leahy
Daniel 'Antrim' Malley	Phelim Drew
Chief Marion O'Hare	Gary Lydon
Thomas 'Lumpy' Flannegan	David Ganly
Mr. Gulliver Sullivan	Declan Conlon
Bobby Boy	Ryan McParland
Mickey No-No	Karl Shiels

SPECIAL THANKS TO

Roadstone Wood Ltd for the provision of concrete for the Drum Belly set.

THANKS ALSO TO

*Paddy, Frank and John at F.X. Buckley's Butchers on Moore Street, Dublin.
Sean Redmond, Eamonn Dunne and Terry Adams from the Parks Division of
Dublin City Council.
John Deegan of Garden Style.*

Please note that the text of the play which appears in this
volume may be changed during the rehearsal process and
appear in a slightly altered form in performance.

Director	Sean Holmes
Set Design	Paul Wills
Lighting Design	Paul Keogan
Costume Design	Eimer Ní Mhaoldomhnaigh
Sound Design	Christopher Shutt
Assistant Director	Maeve Stone
Voice Director	Andrea Ainsworth
Fight Director	Donal O'Farrell
Assistant Set Designer	Adrian Gee
Company Stage Manager	Donna Leonard
Deputy Stage Manager	Róisín Coyle
Assistant Stage Manager	Richie O'Sullivan
Casting Director	Kelly Phelan
Hair and Make-Up	Val Sherlock
Photography	Anthony Woods
Graphic Design	Zero-G
Video Editing	Jack Phelan
Floor Installation	M&P Construction Ltd.
Floor Installation Consultant	John Piggott, Casey O'Rourke Associates.
Set Construction	Theatre Production Services Ltd.
Scenic Finishing	Sandra Butler
Furnace Effect	Se Purcell
Rain Effect	Capital Scenery Ltd
Sign Language Interpreter	Amanda Coogan
Audio Description	Maureen Portsmouth
	Brid Ní Ghruagáin
Captioning	Paula Carraher
	Ruth McCreery

Audio described and captioned performances are provided by Arts and Disability Ireland with funding from the Arts Council of Ireland.

ABBEY THEATRE
DRUM BELLY
RICHARD DORMER

The play is set in Brooklyn, New York, July 1969.

"Exile is a dream of a glorious return. Exile is a vision of revolution...It is an endless paradox: looking forward by always looking back. The exile is a ball hurled high into the air."

Salman Rushdie

RICHARD DORMER
WRITER

THIS IS RICHARD'S DEBUT at the Abbey Theatre. He trained as an actor at the Royal Academy of Dramatic Art in London. He was commissioned to write his first play *Hurricane* in 2002 by Ransom Productions, Belfast. The play went on to win numerous awards and critical acclaim, transferring to the Arts Theatre, West End, London in 2004 and Off Broadway, New York in 2005.

His other plays include *The Half, This Piece of Earth* and *The Gentlemen's Tea-Drinking Society*. Richard's work for Ransom has transferred to the Tron Theatre, Glasgow and has been showcased twice by the British Council in Edinburgh. He recently wrote a libretto called *Driven* for the Northern Ireland Opera.

Richard would like to take this opportunity to thank Rachel O'Riordan for her invaluable encouragement and support of him as a playwright.

Creative Team & Cast

SEAN HOLMES

DIRECTOR

THIS IS SEAN'S DEBUT at the Abbey Theatre. He is Artistic Director of the Lyric Hammersmith where he has worked on *Cinderella, Desire Under the Elms, Morning, Have I None, A Midsummer Night's Dream, Saved, Blasted, A Thousand Stars Explode in the Sky, Ghost Stories, Three Sisters* and *Comedians*. Sean was an Associate Director of the Oxford Stage Company from 2001 to 2006 and has worked for the National Theatre, London and Royal Shakespeare Company as well as the Royal Court, Donmar Warehouse, Tricycle and Chichester Festival Theatre.

PAUL WILLS

SET DESIGN

THIS IS PAUL'S DEBUT at the Abbey Theatre. He works as a set and costume designer and theatre credits include *My Fair Lady, A Number, Sisters* and *Blue/Orange* (Sheffield Theatres), *Buried Child* (Leicester Curve), *Making Noise Quietly* and *Anna Christie*, Olivier Award for Best Revival 2012, *The Man Who Had All the Luck* and *The Cut*, TMA Award for Best Touring Production 2012 (Donmar Warehouse), *Human Being, Di and Viv and Rose* and *The Stock*

Da'wa (Hampstead Theatre), *Orpheus Descending, 1984, Macbeth* and *See How They Run* (Manchester Royal Exchange), *The Acid Test* and *Breathing Corpses* (Royal Court), *The Lightning Child, Dr Faustus, Frontline* and *We The People* (Shakespeare's Globe), *Saved, Punk Rock, The Chair Plays* and *Blasted*, Olivier Award for Outstanding Achievement in an Affiliate Theatre 2011 (Lyric Hammersmith), *Ben Hur* and *Little Voice* (Watermill Theatre), *Novecento* (Donmar Warehouse Season at Trafalgar Studios), *Two Gentlemen of Verona* (Northampton Royal & Derngate), *Waiting for Godot* and *Yerma* (West Yorkshire Playhouse and Talawa Theatre Company), *Serious Money* (Birmingham Rep), *Home* (Theatre Royal Bath), *Pornography* (Tricycle Theatre/Birmingham Rep/Traverse Theatre), *Prometheus Bound* (New York/The Sound Venue), *The Changeling* (English Touring Theatre), *Mammals* (Bush Theatre/UK Tour), *A Kind of Alaska* and *A Slight Ache* (Gate Theatre) and the upcoming *Howie the Rookie* (Project Arts Centre/Irish tour). Work as a set designer includes *The Second Mrs. Tanqueray* and *Treasure Island* (Rose Theatre Kingston) and *The Changeling* and *Mother Courage and her Children* (English Touring Theatre). Work as a costume designer includes *Barnum* (Chichester Festival Theatre) and *Finding Neverland* (Leicester Curve).

Opera credits include *Rusalka* (English Touring Opera), *Sweetness* and *Badness* (Welsh National Opera) and *The Magic Flute* (National Theatre of Palestine).

PAUL KEOGAN

LIGHTING DESIGN

PAUL'S PREVIOUS WORK at the Abbey Theatre includes *Curse of the Starving Class*, *No Romance*, *B for Baby*, *Da*, *No Escape*, *Ages of the Moon*, *The Rivals*, *Marble*, *Lay Me Down Softly*, *The Resistible Rise of Arturo Ui*, *School for Scandal*, *She Stoops to Conquer*, *Romeo and Juliet*, *Woman and Scarecrow*, *Big Love*, *Macbeth*, *The Comedy of Errors*, *Heavenly Bodies*, *The Dandy Dolls*, *Purgatory*, *Chun na Farraige Síos*, *Amazing Grace*, *Julius Caesar*, *The Electrocution of Children*, *Amazing Grace*, *Beauty in a Broken Place*, *The Wild Duck*, *Living Quarters*, *Tartuffe*, *That Was Then*, *The Burial At Thebes*, *The Cherry Orchard*, *Tree Houses*, *Making History*, *The Map Maker's Sorrow*, *Cúirt an Mheán Oíche*, *Mrs Warren's Profession*, *Eden*, *The Morning After Optimism*, *Portia Coughlan*, *The Sanctuary Lamp*, *Bailegangáire*, *Defender of the Faith*, *Down the Line*, *Eden*, *The Tempest*, *Homeland* and *Melonfarmer*. Recent lighting designs include *Tiny Plays For Ireland 1 and 2* (Fishamble: The New Play Company), *Romeo and Juliet* (Corcadorca), *The Last Summer* and

A Woman of No Importance (Gate Theatre), *Big Maggie, Penelope* and *The Walworth Farce* (Druid), *Angel/Babel* (Operating Theatre, Dublin), *Snegurochka* (Wexford Festival Opera), *The Barber of Seville* (Cork Opera House), *Lady Macbeth of Mtensk, The Silver Tassie* and *Dead Man Walking* (Opera Ireland), *Mixed Marriage* (Lyric Theatre, Belfast), *Before it Rains* (Sherman Cymru and Bristol Old Vic), *Eugene Onegin*, *Idomeneo* and *Pique Dame* (Grange Park Opera), *The Misanthrope* and *A Streetcar Named Desire* (Playhouse, Liverpool), *Semele* (Royal Irish Academy of Music), *La Bohème* and *Wake* (Nationale Reisopera, Netherlands), *Yerma* (West Yorkshire Playhouse), *Novecento* (Trafalgar Studios), *Intemperance* (Everyman, Liverpool), *The Taming of the Shrew* (Royal Shakespeare Company), *Harvest* (Royal Court Theatre), *The Stock Da'Wa* (Hampstead Theatre), *Blue/Orange* (Crucible Theatre), *Pierrot Lunaire* (Almeida Theatre), *Trad* (Galway Arts Festival), *Man of Aran Re-Imagined* (Once Off Productions), *The Makropulos Case* and *Der Fliegende Holländer* (Opera Zuid, Netherlands) and *Die Zauberflöte* (National Opera of Korea). Paul studied Drama at Trinity College, Dublin and at Glasgow University.

EIMER NÍ MHAOLDOMHNAIGH

COSTUME DESIGN

EIMER'S PREVIOUS WORK at the Abbey Theatre includes *Shibari* and *Made in China*. Recent work includes *Half a Glass* and *Farewell* (Field Day Theatre Company), *Words of Advice for Young People, Take Me Away, Don Carlos, Solemn Mass for a Full Moon in Summer* and *The Importance of Being Earnest* (Rough Magic Theatre Company), *Little Women* and *Hay Fever* (Gate Theatre), *Benefactors* (b*spoke theatre company) and *Translations* (Hands Turn Theatre Company). Film and television credits include the upcoming *Calvary, The Guard, Neverland, Leap Year, Ondine, Breakfast on Pluto, Brideshead Revisited, Becoming Jane, Omagh, The Wind that Shakes the Barley*, which won the 2006 Palme d'Or Award at Cannes, *Alarm, About Adam, Timbuktu* and *In America*. As Assistant Designer, Eimer worked on *Michael Collins, The Butcher Boy, An Awfully Big Adventure* and *Family*. Eimer has also styled commercials for Eircom, RSA, Vodafone, AIB, Hibernian Aviva, Barnardos, Bulmers, Irish Rail, Eircom and MasterCard. She is a lecturer in Dun Laoghaire Institute of Art Design & Technology on the Design for Stage and Screen degree course. Eimer is a graduate of Limerick School of Art and Design. She has been nominated for an Emmy, a Satellite award and has received five IFTA nominations.

CHRISTOPHER SHUTT

SOUND DESIGN

THIS IS CHRISTOPHER'S DEBUT at the Abbey Theatre. He is an Artistic Associate at the Bristol Old Vic. Recent theatre work includes *War Horse* (West End, Broadway, Canada, Australia, US Tour, Berlin) for which he received a 2011 Tony Award for Best Sound Design, *The Effect, Timon of Athens, The Last of the Haussmans, Comedy of Errors, Emperor and Galilean, The White Guard, Or You Could Kiss Me, Burnt by the Sun, Every Good Boy Deserves Favour, Gethsemane, The Hour We Knew Nothing of Each Other, Philistines, Happy Days, Coram Boy* (also Broadway), *A Dream Play, Measure for Measure, Mourning Becomes Electra, The PowerBook, Humble Boy, Play Without Words, Hamlet, Albert Speer, Not About Nightingales, Chips with Everything, The Homecoming* and *Machinal* (National Theatre, London). Other theatre work includes *A Disappearing Number, The Elephant Vanishes, A Minute Too Late, Mnemonic, Noise of Time, Street of Crocodiles, Three Lives of Lucie Cabrol* and *Caucasian Chalk Circle*

(Complicite), *The Tempest, Twelfth Night, King Lear, Much Ado About Nothing, King John* and *Romeo and Juliet* (Royal Shakespeare Company), *The Playboy of the Western World, All About My Mother* and *Moon for the Misbegotten* (Old Vic, London, Broadway), *Philadelphia, Here I Come!, Piaf, Hecuba* and *The Man Who Had All The Luck* (Donmar Warehouse, London), *Ruined* and *Judgment Day* (Almeida), *Love & Information, Kin, Aunt Dan and Lemon, Serious Money* and *Road* (Royal Court, London), *The Caretaker* and *Bull* (Sheffield Crucible), *Far Away* and *A Midsummer Night's Dream* (Bristol Old Vic), *All My Sons* (Broadway), *The Bacchae* and *Little Otik* (National Theatre of Scotland) and *The Resistible Rise of Arturo Ui* (New York). Radio work includes *A Shropshire Lad, Tennyson's Maud, A Disappearing Number* and *After the Quake* (BBC). He previously won New York Drama Desk Awards for *War Horse, Mnemonic* and *Not About Nightingales.* He has also received Olivier Award nominations for *Coram Boy, War Horse, Piaf* and *Every Good Boy Deserves Favour.*

MAEVE STONE
RESIDENT ASSISTANT DIRECTOR

MAEVE IS RESIDENT Assistant Director at the Abbey Theatre and has worked with Selina Cartmell on *King Lear,* Joe Dowling on *The Dead* and Wayne Jordan on *The Plough and the Stars.* She co-founded Spilt Gin with playwright James Hickson and has directed and toured several plays since 2009 including *Andy Warhol's Nothing Special* (Project Arts Centre and Belltable Arts Centre) and *Taste* (Project Arts Centre and Solstice at Cork Midsummer Festival). Recently she directed and dramaturged the collaboratively written *You Can't Just Leave - There's Always Something* (Spilt Gin, Site Specific) which was nominated for Best New Writing, Best Off-Site Production and Spirit of the Fringe at the ABSOLUT Fringe Awards 2011. Recent assistant directing credits include *Everyone is King Lear in his own Home* and *A Doll House* (Pan Pan, Smock Alley). Originally from Limerick, she graduated from Trinity College, Dublin with a B.A. in Theatre and English in 2009.

DONAL O'FARRELL
FIGHT DIRECTOR

DONAL'S PREVIOUS WORK at the Abbey Theatre includes *King Lear, Quietly, The Government Inspector, Lovers at Versailles, The Big House, Hamlet, Portia Coughlan, Chun na Farraige Síos, Defender of the Faith, Purgatory, The Dandy Dolls, I Do Not Like Thee, Dr Fell, The*

Shaughraun, *The House of Bernarda Alba*, *Henry IV*, *The Sanctuary Lamp*, *The Morning After Optimism*, *A Whistle in the Dark*, *A Life*, *The Wake* and *The Honey Spike*. Other theatre productions include *Drive By* (Cork City Docks), *Done Up Like a Kipper*, *Juno and the Paycock* and *Maria* (Wexford Festival Opera) and *The Field* (SFX Theatre). Donal has worked as a stunt co-ordinator on films including *Frank*, *Gold*, *The F Word*, *Byzantium*, *Good Vibrations*, *Shadow Dancer*, *Citadel*, *Whole Lotta Sole*, *Hidden*, *The Guard*, *My Brothers*, *Runway*, *Happy Ever Afters*, *Triage*, *Cracks*, *The Daisy Chain*, *Becoming Jane*, *The Tiger's Tale*, *Mighty Celt*, *Sanctuary*, *Flowers of Desire*, *Zonad*, *P.S. I Love You* and *Lassie*. Television work as a stunt co-ordinator includes *Line of Duty 2*, *Single Handed*, *Love/Hate* and *Raw* (RTÉ), *Life of Crime*, *Quirke*, *The Ice Cream Girls*, *The Fall*, *Hidden*, *Scup*, *Titanic: Blood and Steel*, *Rásaí na Gaillimhe*, *Vexed*, *Neverland*, *Jack Taylor*, *Primeval*, *Treasure Island*, *George Gently* and *Murphy's Law*. Donal has also worked as a fight director for the Gaiety Theatre, SFX Theatre and Project Arts Centre.

LIAM CARNEY
HARVEY MARR

LIAM'S PREVIOUS WORK at the Abbey Theatre includes *Tales of Ballycumber*, *The Seafarer*, *The Playboy of the Western World*, *Romeo and Juliet*, *Homeland*, *Portia Coughlan*, *Done Up Like A Kipper*, *The Passion of Jerome*, *Twenty Grand*, *A Picture of Paradise* and *Brothers of the Brush*. Other theatre work includes *The Silver Tassie* and *The Cripple of Inishmaan* (Druid), *There Came A Gypsy Riding* (Livin' Dred Theatre Company), *Cruel and Tender* (Project Arts Centre), *A Dublin Carol* (Everyman Palace Theatre), *Frozen* (Tall Tales), *Mud* (Corn Exchange), *All's Well That Ends Well* (Classic Stage), *Studs* (Gaiety Theatre), *Bedbound* (Corcadorca) and *We Ourselves*, *Kitchensink* and *Buddlea* (Passion Machine). Film and television work includes *Speed Dating* (System Forty Eight Ltd), *Studs* (Brother Films), *Spin the Bottle* (Filmove Studio), *Martin* (Celtic Mouse Productions), *Tupperware* (Irish Film Board), *Gangs of New York* (Miramax Films), *When The Sky Falls* (Entertainment International), *Angela's Ashes* (DB Productions), *Soft Sand Blue Sea* (Channel 4 Films), *The Boxer* (Hell's Kitchen), *Braveheart* (Icon Entertainment), *The Commitments* (Beacon Communications), *Life of Crime* and *The Ambassador* (Ecosse), *Ripper Street*, *The Hanging Gale* and

Ballykissangel (BBC), *Titanic Blood and Steel* (Titanic Films), *Jack Taylor* (Finder Films), *The Clinic* (Parallel Films), *Single Handed, Glenroe* and *Pure Mule* (RTÉ) and *Sharpe* (Carlton TV).

GERARD BYRNE
WALTER SORROW

GERARD'S PREVIOUS WORK at the Abbey Theatre includes *The Picture of Dorian Gray, Arrah-na-Pogue, The Shaughraun, Tarry Flynn, Observe the Sons of Ulster Marching Towards the Somme, Macbeth, Strange Occurrence on Ireland's Eye, Frauds* and *Blinded by the Light.* Other theatre work includes *Home, Buddleia, War, Brownbread, Studs* and *The Birdtable* (The Passion Machine Theatre Company), *Emma, Silas Marner* and *Esther Waters* (Storytellers Theatre Company), *The Carnival King* (Fishamble: The New Play Company), *The Pope and the Witch* (Red Kettle), *West Side Story* (Olympia Theatre), *Summerhouse* (Druid), *The Man with the Flower in his Mouth, Impressions of Vincent Van Gogh, The Man in the Iron Mask* and *The Man who Cared too Much* (Project Arts Centre), *Trojan Women* (Smock Alley Theatre), *What's Left of the Flag,* Irish Times Theatre Awards nomination for Best New Play 2010 (Theatre Upstairs) and *Overtime* (New Theatre). Film and television

work includes *Before I Sleep* and *Tupperware* (Brother Films), *Crush Proof* (Continent Film GmbH), *After Midnight* (Channel 4 Films), *The Truth About Claire* and *Fair City* (RTÉ), *The Snapper* (BBC Films), *Noreen* (Domhnall Gleeson) and *Happy Birthday Oscar Wilde* (Mind the Gap Films). He was actor/presenter of the documentary *A Matter Of Life And Debt* (Radharc and RTÉ). Radio work includes *The Hit List* (RTÉ). Gerard has also worked and toured extensively in the UK and Europe. He has worked in both the Edinburgh Fringe and Edinburgh International Festivals, the Bonner Biennale Festival in Germany and the l'Imaginaire Irlandais festival at Théâtre de l'Europe in Paris.

CIARÁN O'BRIEN
JOHNNY 'THE FOX' ROURKE

CIARÁN'S PREVIOUS WORK at the Abbey Theatre includes *The Government Inspector, Curse of the Starving Class, Perve, Arrah-na-Pogue, The Plough and the Stars* (2010), *The Comedy of Errors, The Resistible Rise of Arturo Ui, Saved, Julius Caesar* and *The Importance of Being Earnest.* Other theatre work includes *Elevator* (THISISPOPBABY), *The Great Goat Bubble* (Fishamble: The New Play Company), *Travesties* (Rough Magic Theatre Company), *Durang Durang* (Project Arts Centre),

Between Foxrock and a Hard Place
(Landmark Productions), *The
Shawshank Redemption* (Gaiety
Theatre, Cork Opera House and Derry
Millennium Forum), *Philadelphia,
Here I Come!* (Gaiety Theatre), *Observe
the Sons of Ulster Marching Towards
the Somme* (Livin' Dred Theatre
Company and Nomad), *This is Our
Youth* (Bedrock Productions), *Peter
Pan* (Pavilion Theatre), *The Magic Tee*
(Granary Theatre, Edinburgh Fringe,
Belltable Theatre, Dublin Fringe), *Lil'
Red and Sk8er Jack* (Civic Theatre),
Fewer Emergencies (Randolph SD
| The Company), *How Many Miles
to Babylon?* (Second Age Theatre
Company), *Myrmidons* (Ouroboros
Theatre Company), *Seven Deadly
Teens* (Dublin Fringe Festival) and
Oliver Twist (Gate Theatre). Film
and television work includes *The
Last Security Man* (RTÉ Storyland),
The Tudors (Showtime Networks),
Fair City and *Custer's Last Stand Up*
(RTÉ), *Detained* (Zombies Don't Run),
Bloom (Odyssey Pictures), *Prince
William* (Fox Television Studios),
Incredible Story Studio (Minds Eye
Entertainment) and *The Boy from
Mercury* (Blue Rose Films). Ciarán
is a graduate of Bachelor of Acting
Studies, Samuel Beckett Centre Trinity
College, Dublin.

RONAN LEAHY
WILLY 'WICKLOW' HILL

RONAN'S PREVIOUS WORK at the
Abbey Theatre includes *King Lear,
Curse of the Starving Class, Macbeth,
The Resistible Rise of Arturo Ui, Romeo
and Juliet, Henry IV (Part I), Da,
Living Quarters, Observatory, The
Passion of Jerome, At Swim Two Birds,
By the Bog of Cats, Observe the Sons of
Ulster Marching Towards the Somme,
Monkey, The Man Who Became a
Legend, The Adventures of Shay
Mouse, Philadelphia, Here I Come!,
The Doctor's Dilemma, The Well of
the Saints* and *The Corsican Brothers.*
Other theatre work includes *Festen* and
All My Sons (Gate Theatre), *Travesties,
Life is a Dream* and *Solemn Mass for a
Full Moon in Summer* (Rough Magic
Theatre Company), *Gentrification*
(Druid), *The Winter's Tale* and *The
Hairy Ape* (Corcadorca), *Medea, Titus
Andronicus* and *La Musica* (Siren
Productions), *Moment* (Tall Tales), *The
Case of the Rose Tattoo* and *La Marea*
(Dublin Theatre Festival), *Gagarin
Way* (Island), *Pyrenees* (Hatch Theatre
Company), *Frozen* (Cork Opera House),
Roberto Zucco, Pale Angel and *Wideboy
Gospel* (Bedrock Productions), *The
End of the Road, Whereabouts* and *The
Flesh Addict* (Fishamble: The New Play
Company), *The Chairs* (Tinderbox),
Melon Farmer (Theatre Royal
Plymouth), *Russian Tales* and *White*

Woman Street (Meridian), *Mister Staines* (Pan Pan), *Carshow* (Corn Exchange), *Easter Dues* (Bickerstaffe), *Romeo and Juliet* (Second Age Theatre Company), *Kiss of the Spider Woman* (Tin Drum) and *A Fine Day for a Hunt* (Punchbag). Television and film work includes *Jack Taylor* (Magma), *Amber* (Screenworks), *Angel* (Ruán Mangan), *Single-Handed*, *A Fair City Special* and *On Home Ground* (RTÉ), *Coolockland* (RTÉ Short Cuts) *Blood Coloured Moon* (Filmbase/RTÉ), *Roy* (BBC/Jam media), *The Catalpa Rescue* (CIS TV Australia), *The Ghosts of Duffy's Cut* (RTÉ/Tile Films), *Batman Begins* (Warner Bros. Pictures), *Proof* (RTÉ/Subotica) and *Amongst Women* (BBC/RTÉ). Directing credits include *After Miss Julie* (Purpleheart), *Tara Has Written A Play*, *The Journey* and *All the Glove in the World* (Fishamble Shorts), *Little Malcolm and his Struggle Against the Eunuchs*, *Free Range* and *The Girl Who Barked like a Dog* (Bull Alley), *Titus Andronicus* (Assistant/Siren), *Mud* (Assistant/Corn Exchange) and *Urban Ghost* (Assistant/Bedrock).

PHELIM DREW
DANIEL 'ANTRIM' MALLEY

PHELIM'S PREVIOUS WORK at the Abbey Theatre includes *King Lear*, *Bookworms* (2012 & 2010), *Curse of the Starving Class*, *The Seafarer*, *The Rivals*, *The Playboy of the Western World*, *Three Sisters*, *The Crucible*, *A Doll's House*, *The Shaughraun*, *Portia Coughlan*, *Heavenly Bodies*, *The Cherry Orchard*, *Whistle in the Dark*, *The Corsican Brothers*, *The Plough and the Stars* and *Blinded by the Light*. Other theatre work includes *Port Authority* (Decadent Theatre), *The Making of 'Tis Pity She's A Whore* (Siren Productions), *All That Fall* (Pan Pan Theatre), *Sleeping Beauty* (Landmark Productions), *2 Rooms* (Focus Theatre), *Operation Easter* (Calipso), *Hinterland* (Out of Joint), *Thérèse Raquin*, *A Christmas Carol*, *Weeping of Angels*, *She Stoops to Conquer*, *Pride and Prejudice*, *Present Laughter*, *The Double Dealer* and *Tartuffe* (Gate Theatre), *The Plough and the Stars* (Gaiety Theatre), *Galileo* (Almedia Theatre), *The Dream* (Lyceum Theatre), *Love and a Bottle* (Rough Magic Theatre Company), *Cheapside* (Druid) and *As You Like It* (Tivoli Theatre). Film and television work includes *The Escapist* (SCR Productions), *King Arthur* (Disney), *Into the West* (Channel 4 Films), *The Commitments* (Beacon Communications), *My Left Foot* (Palace), *In Like Flynn* (Subotica Films), *An Crisis* and *Anseo* (Wildfire Films), *Val Falvey, TD* (Grand Pictures), *No Laughing Matter*, *The Clinic* and *Making the Cut* (RTÉ), *Rough Diamond* (BBC) and *The Big Bow Wow* (Parallel Films).

GARY LYDON
CHIEF MARION O'HARE

GARY'S PREVIOUS WORK at the Abbey Theatre includes *Lay Me Down Softly*, *A Whistle in the Dark*, *The House*, *Translations*, *The Cavalcaders*, *Conversations on a Homecoming* and *The Wexford Trilogy*. Other theatre work includes *The Last Summer* and *Pygmalion* (Gate Theatre), *The Normal Heart* and *The Young Europeans* (Project Arts Centre), *Sive*, *Tinkers Wedding*, *Well of the Saints* and *The Playboy of the Western World* (Druid), *Trumpet and Raspberries*, *The Fire Raisers*, *What The Butler Saw* and *Fool For Love* (Wexford Theatre Co-operative), *Lay Me Down Softly* and *The Wexford Trilogy* (Tricycle Theatre), *The Playboy of the Western World* (Old Vic), *Dublin Carol* (Donmar at Trafalgar Studios), *One Is Not A Number* (Meridian Theatre Company), *The Cripple of Inishmaan* and *The Walls* (Royal National Theatre), *The Wexford Trilogy*, *Belfry*, *Poor Beast in the Rain*, *Handful of Stars* (Bush Theatre) and *Same Old Moon* (Nuffield Theatre, Southampton). Film and television work includes *Bramwell* (ITV), *The Wexford Trilogy* (BBC), *Hard Cases* (Central), *The Bill* (Thames), *Seaforth* (Initial), *The Clinic*, Winner IFTA for Best Supporting Actor 2005 and 2007, *Pure Mule*, *A Soldier's Song*
and *On Home Ground* (RTÉ), *Stella Days* (Newgrange Pictures), *War Horse* (Dreamworks), *The Guard* (Element Pictures), *Fergus's Wedding* (Grand Pictures), *Last September* (Trimark Pictures), *Michael Collins* (Warner Bros. Pictures), *Strapless* (Strapless Films), *Country* (Indi Films), *Ordinary Decent Criminal* (Icon Entertainment), *Nothing Personal* (Channel 4 Films) and the upcoming *Calvary* (Octagon Films) and *Gold* (Subotica Films).

DAVID GANLY
THOMAS 'LUMPY' FLANNEGAN

DAVID'S PREVIOUS WORK at the Abbey Theatre includes *The Cavalcaders*, *Observe the Sons of Ulster Marching Towards the Somme* and *Philadelphia, Here I Come!*. Other theatre work includes *The Weir* (Gate Theatre), *The Risen People* and *The Snow Queen* (Gaiety Theatre), *Grease*, *The Sound of Music* and *The Wizard of Oz* (Olympia Theatre), *The Plough and the Stars* (Second Age Theatre Company), *Extremities* (Andrew's Lane Theatre), *Carousel* (Tivoli Theatre), *Shoot the Crow* and *Summerhouse* (Druid), *F!* (Dublin Theatre Festival), *Amphibians* (YMCA, Wexford), *The Merchant of Venice* (Lyric Theatre, Belfast), *Cinderella* (Lyric Hammersmith), *Macbeth* (Crucible Theatre, Sheffield),

Of Mice and Men (The Watermill, Newbury), *The Wizard Of Oz* (London Palladium), *Beauty Queen of Leenane, Bedtime Story & The End of the Beginning* (Young Vic), *Chicago* (Cambridge Theatre), *The Wizard of Oz* (West Yorkshire Playhouse), *The Field, The Cavalcaders* and *John Bull's Other Island* (Tricycle Theatre), *Translations* (National Theatre, London), *Hamlet, The Weir* and *Waiting for Godot* (Theatre Royal, Northampton), *Americans, The Contractor* and *The Quare Fellow* (Oxford Stage Company), *The Full Monty* (Prince of Wales Theatre), *The Lonesome West* (Druid, Royal Court, Sydney and Broadway), *Russian Tales* and *The Cavalcaders* (Meridian Theatre Company), *The Talented Mr Ripley* (Watford Theatre) and *Dancing at Lughnasa* (Salisbury Playhouse). Film and television work includes *Body of Lies* (Warner Bros. Pictures), *Hippie Hippie Shake* (Studio Canal), *Dorothy Mills* (Fidélite Prouctions), *Widow's Peak* (British Screen Productions), *Doctors* (BBC) and *Upwardly Mobile* (RTÉ).

DECLAN CONLON
MR. GULLIVER SULLIVAN

DECLAN'S PREVIOUS WORK at the Abbey Theatre includes *Quietly, The House,* Winner Irish Times Theatre Award for Best

Actor 2012, *Terminus* (national and international tour), Manchester Theatre Awards nomination for Best Actor 2011, *The Last Days of a Reluctant Tyrant, A Whistle in the Dark, Famine, The Patriot Game, The Burial at Thebes, The Crucible, The Recruiting Officer, Julius Caesar, A Month in The Country,* Winner Irish Times Theatre Award for Best Supporting Actor 2006, *True West, The Hamlet Project, All My Sons, Henry IV (Part 1), Heavenly Bodies, What Happened Bridgie Cleary* and *The Last Ones.* Other theatre work includes *The Last Summer, The Book of Evidence* (originally produced in conjunction with Kilkenny Arts Festival) and *The Importance of Being Earnest* (Gate Theatre), *The Sanctuary Lamp* (b*spoke theatre company), *Improbable Frequency* and *Copenhagen,* Irish Times Theatre Award nomination for Best Actor 2002 (Rough Magic Theatre Company), *Miss Julie* (Landmark Productions) and *The Country* (Arclight), *As You Like It, The Spanish Tragedy, La Lupa, The Mysteries* and *Henry VI* (Royal Shakespeare Company), *The Walls, The Ends of the Earth* and *The Machine Wreckers* (National Theatre, London), *Macbeth* (West End), *Our Country's Good* (Young Vic) and *Uncle Vanya* (Lyric Theatre, Belfast). Television credits include *The Tudors* (Showtime), *Single*

Handed (RTÉ and ITV), *Amber,
Raw, Trouble in Paradise, Proof* and
Bachelors Walk (RTÉ), *Anytime Now,
Dangerfield* and *The Family* (BBC) and
Cromwell (Title Films). Film credits
include *Debris, Hereafter, Trouble with
Sex, Honest* and *All Souls Day.* Radio
work includes *The Burial at Thebes*
and *The Hounds of the Baskerville.*

RYAN MCPARLAND
BOBBY BOY

THIS IS RYAN'S DEBUT on the
Abbey stage. He previously appeared
in *Half a Glass of Water* by David
Ireland which was part of *Something
Borrowed,* the 2011 Short Play
Readings on the Peacock stage. Other
theatre work includes *Doughnuts*
(TEAM), *The Civilisation Game*
(Lyric Theatre, Belfast), *One Tribe*
(Spanner in the Works) and *Choices*
(C21 Northern Ireland tour). Radio
work includes *The Biggest Issues* and
Loves Worst Day (BBC Radio 4).
Film and television credits includes
Fishbowl City (DBS Productions),
6 Degrees (BBC), *SLR* (SLR Films),
Igloo (MFD Films), *Imbolc* and *Say
Nothing* (NI Screen), *Coming Up –
Spoof Or Die* (Channel 4) and *Good
Vibrations* (Canderblinks). Ryan
is currently developing a Northern
Ireland truth and reconciliation play
with American director Michael
Lessac for Global Arts Corps.

KARL SHIELS
MICKEY NO-NO

KARL'S PREVIOUS WORK at the
Abbey Theatre includes *The House,
Macbeth, Terminus* (Edinburgh
Festival Fringe), *The Comedy of
Errors, The Resistible Rise of Arturo
Ui, Romeo and Juliet, Howie the
Rookie, Beauty in a Broken Place,
Henry IV (Part I), Barbaric Comedies,
At Swim-Two-Birds* and *Twenty
Grand.* Other theatre work includes
The Death of Harry Leon, Irish Times
Theatre Award nomination for Best
Supporting Actor 2009 (Smock Alley
Theatre), *Hue and Cry* (Bewley's Café
Theatre, Oran Mor and Glasgow), *The
Pride of Parnell Street* (Fishamble:
The New Play Company), *Howie the
Rookie* (Bush Theatre), *Penelope,*
Stage Award nomination for Best
Actor 2010 and Irish Times Theatre
Award nomination for Best Actor 2011
(Druid), *Oedipus Loves You* and *Hamlet*
(Pan Pan), *Sleeping Beauty* (Helix),
Salomé (Gate Theatre), *Greek, Quartet,
Muller's Medea, Obituary, Early
Morning, This Lime Tree Bower, The
Massacre @ Paris, Fully Recovered,
The Spanish Tragedy* and *The Duchess
of Malfi* (Project Arts Centre), *Venus
and Adonis* (Samuel Beckett Centre),
Comedians, Dublin Theatre Festival
Award for Best Actor 1999 (Dublin
Theatre Festival), *The Shadow of a
Gunman* (Lyric Theatre, Belfast) and

Duck (Royal Court). Karl is Artistic Director of Semper Fi, where he has directed *Adrenalin, God's Grace, Ladies and Gents*, Edinburgh Fringe First Award 2004, *Ten, Slaughter, Breakfast with Versace, Within 24 Hours, Another 24 Hours, Within 24 Hours of Dance, Conversation with a Cupboard Man* and *Butterflies*. He also directed *The Dark Room (Gentle Giant), Topdog/Underdog* and *Three Tall Women* (Tall Tales Theatre Company), *Drapes, Eggshell* and *Bernard Opens Up* (Fishamble: The New Play Company), *Gargarin Way* (Island Theatre Company), *The Pitchfork Disney* and *Fallen* (Raw Image). Film and television credits include *At Death's Door* (Warrior Films), *Savage* (SP Films), *Titanic: Blood and Steel* (DAP), *Haywire* (Relativity Media), *Eden* (Samson Films), *W.C.* (Hyper Films), *Prosperity* (Element Films), *Batman Begins* (Warner Bros. Pictures), *Intermission* (Brown Sauce Film Productions), *Spin the Bottle* (Grand Pictures), *Get Rich or Die Tryin'* (Paramount Pictures), *Veronica Guerin* (Touchstone Pictures), *Mystics* (Essex Film Productions Ltd), *Freaky Deaky 10/1* and *Meeting Che Guevera and the Man from Maybury Hill* (Igloo Films), *Trafficked*, Best Actor IFTA nomination 2002 (New Decade TV and Film), *The Tudors, Doctors, Peaky Blinders* and *Shadowdancer* (BBC), *Attachments* (World Productions),

Waiting for Dublin (Corsan), *Virtues of a Sinner* (Curved Street Films), *The Anarchic Hand Affair* (RTÉ and Princess Pictures), *The Clinic, Private Lives, Camera Café, On Home Ground* and *Butchers* (RTÉ), *Any Time Now* (Comet Productions), *Stitches* (Fantastic Films), *Foyle's War* (ITV), *No Justice* (Bootstrap Films), *Blonde* (BFilms), *Angel* (Angel Films) and *Noble* (Noble Films). Karl is the Artistic Director of Theatre Upstairs and received a Special Judges' Award as part of the Irish Times Theatre Awards 2012 for his commitment to the development and promotion of emerging artists in Irish theatre.

The Abbey Theatre would like to thank the supporters of the 110th Anniversary Campaign 1904–2014

'We have established the Abbey Theatre's 110th Anniversary Fund to ensure we continue to fuel the flame our founders lit over a century ago. I am proud to be a supporter of the 110th Campaign by being a Guardian of the Abbey Theatre. With your support we can develop playwrights, support Ireland's theatre artists, engage Irish citizens and present world renowned theatre both nationally and internationally.'

Fiach Mac Conghail, Director / Stiúrthóir

CORPORATE GUARDIANS

The Doyle Collection, official hotel partner of Ireland's national theatre.

McCann FitzGerald ARTHUR COX

Bank of Ireland BROWN THOMAS AON

  Irish Life   SIPTU

MEDIA PARTNERS

Sunday Independent

Irish Independent

SUPPORTER OF THE NEW PLAYWRIGHTS PROGRAMME

Deloitte.

CORPORATE AMBASSADORS

Paddy Power
101 Talbot Restaurant
Bewley's
Wynn's Hotel
Abbey Travel
CRH
Conway Communications
Lafayette Cafe
Bar & Gallery
The Merrion Hotel
Baker Tilly Ryan Glennon
National Radio Cabs
The Church Café Bar
Clarion Consulting
Limited
Westin Hotels & Resorts
Manor House Hotels
of Ireland
Zero-G
Irish Poster Advertising
Bad Ass Café

CORPORATE AMBASSADORS

Spector Information
Security
ely bar & brasserie
University College Cork

CORPORATE PARTNERS

AIB
High Performance
Management

SUPPORTING CAST

Anraí Ó Braonáin
Joe Byrne
Robbi D. Holman
Susan McGrath
Oonagh Desire
Róise Goan
John Daly
Zita Byrne

GUARDIANS OF THE ABBEY

Mrs. Carmel Naughton
Sen. Fiach Mac Conghail

FELLOWS OF THE ABBEY

Frances Britton
Catherine Byrne
Sue Cielinski
Dónall Curtin
Tommy Gibbons
James Hickey
John Keane
Andrew Mackey
Eugene Magee
James McNally
Donal Moore
Pat Moylan
Elizabeth Purcell Cribbin
Marie Rogan &
Paul Moore

Abbey Theatre
Staff & Supporters

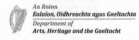

An Roinn
Ealaíon, Oidhreachta agus Gaeltachta
Department of
Arts, Heritage and the Gaeltacht

The Abbey Theatre gratefully acknowledges the financial
support of the Arts Council of Ireland and the support of the
Department of the Arts, Heritage and the Gaeltacht.

Archive partner of the Abbey Theatre.

Dedicated to the memory of
Robert Anthony Welch
1947–2013
Poet, Novelist, Playwright, Black Belt Shodan

Drum Belly

'Exile is a dream of a glorious return. Exile is
a vision of revolution . . . It is an endless paradox:
looking forward by always looking back. The exile
is a ball hurled high into the air.'

Salman Rushdie

Characters

Harvey Marr, *sixties*
Walter Sorrow, *sixties*
Chief Marion O'Hare, *fifties*
Johnny 'The Fox' Rourke, *twenty-five*
Willy 'Wicklow' Hill, *thirties*
Daniel 'Antrim' Malley, *thirties*
Thomas 'Lumpy' Flannegan, *forties*
Mickey No-No, *thirties*
Gulliver Sullivan, *fifties*
Bobby Boy, *sixteen*

The play is set in Brooklyn, New York, July 1969.

Prologue

Darkness.

John F. Kennedy's voice rings out. It is the recording of his 1961 address to the American nation from Texas.

JFK (*voice-over*)   We choose to go to the moon . . .

Applause and cheering.

JFK (*voice-over*)   . . . We choose to go to the moon, we choose to go to the moon in this decade and do the other things, not because they are easy but because they are hard, because that goal will serve to organise and measure the best of our energies and skills. Because that challenge is one we are willing to accept, one we are unwilling to postpone and one we intend to win . . . and the others too.

A roar of an appreciative crowd, deafening.

Music: '1969' by The Stooges. This fades to silence.

The dark continues.

Gently, a baritone male voice begins to hum the hymn 'Abide with Me'.

Then, the soft wet sound of someone sawing meat.

After several long moments the lights come up slowly on . . .

The basement.

The bowels of a ten-storey Brooklyn tenement building. A sturdy wooden table upstage centre. A naked hanging light bulb dimly illuminates the scene. It is so dark that the walls are barely discernible. The table and floor are covered in sheets of cellophane plastic. There is blood everywhere. The bulk of an old furnace water-heating system lurks in the shadows. **Walter Sorrow**, *a big bald man in a bloodied white butcher's apron over a blue pinstripe suit, stands with his back to us. He is cutting up large lumps of some unidentifiable hairless animal with a handsaw. Every now and then he disposes of a piece of meat and bone in one of the several metal buckets beneath the table. Another man stands nearby*

*in an ill-fitting black suit and a pork-pie hat smoking a cigarette: the
weathered but irrepressible* **Harvey Marr**.

Walter *hums the hymn whilst he works. He continues throughout the
following.*

Harvey   . . . We work a goddam miracle, and what thanks?
We go to the moon, we paint the Sistine Chapel, we put a
bullet in a guy's face. It's work. Extraordinary things happen
every day. We get up. Go to bed. Unfuckinbelievable. All the
things in between? Even more extraordinary. We do it. Huh?
We do it. We keep doin' it. Man's gotta eat. I gotta grand-
daughter. Mother's a junkie. Kids gotta eat. You're OK, Walter.
Yes you are. Sullivan? He's a good man. Best pal. Johnny?
Good kid. Yes. But some people? These rip-shits? Get treated
like normal people? Where's the sense in that? Hunks a' shit.
Some people? Don't deserve to live. Take up too much space.
(*To the buckets under the table.*) Ya fuck. (*To* **Walter.**) Wanna
smoke? (*To the buckets.*) Pig fuck . . . (*To* **Walter.**) I'll bet he had
to break his shit up with a fuckin' pole. Size twelve feet.
European measurement. You know what they say? Big feet?
Big shits. Details. That's life. The devil's in it. Wouldn't flush.
Yes sir, Mr Sorrow. The world's a better place. How's your
mother? . . . That bad . . . I'm sorry, Sorrow. Fuck that. Life
is . . . poof . . . She a religious woman? . . . It'll see her
through. Yes. Take me, I ain't religious an' all or anythin' but I
get moments. Clarity. You could say I have epiphanies. Dizzy
Jesus. What a day. Tits on 'er like wet paper bags. Idiot! You're
an idiot, Harvey! The day I've had, Walter, you wouldn't
believe. Everything, it's . . . The fuckin' day. *Postmen?* Let me
tell ya. You wouldn't think to look at me but today I had a skin
full. A belly full a' bourbon, Walter, Kentucky fire water. Two
bottles, maybe fuckin' three. Broad liked her bourbon. Christ.
Told me she was forty-nine . . . she wasn't. (*Pause.*) Her
daughter might a' been. I told her as much. She starts
screaming the place like bejesus. Ya know? Hysterical, like her
fanny's on fire. I gotta get outta here. Spill on to the sidewalk
like a bucket of sick. I'm a shambles. I'm staggering about the
street like a fuckin' prophet. I'm arguing with myself. 'S true.

I'm convinced now that I'm my own father, God rest the mick son of a bitch. I never knew the bastard, but he must have existed. And I'm havin' a pop at him for turning out such a fuck-up of a human being, which is me. So I'm both, you see? It's fuckin' *epic*. It's . . . at one point I'm actually, I may have been crying. Shameful. I know. It's fucked-up. And then I'm loosing control of my bladder, Walter. A piss buster's comin' on. A loo-loo. I'm feeling a trickle. The beginnings of a gush. So I run to the side of the street, ya know, dignity an' all, I run to the side of the street, into an alley, under this tree or somethin' or a lamp post or somethin' and I whack it out, ya know. Out comes Johnny Thomas. Zzzipp. Flumpff. Whoosh. Ahhh. It's good. Fucking notable. So. So far so so-so . . . an' during this little interlude I look down and see what I'm zizzin' on. An' ya know what it is? . . . It's a gnome. Ya know? Those fuckin' garden things? Those things that people do? And it's big. It's a monster. About so high. Up to my nut sack. What's that about? People are fucked. Generally. Fuckos. But fuck that. I'm good. Man's landing on the moon, for Christ sakes.

Pause.

I hope you're getting all this, Walter?

Walter *becomes silent. He stops sawing meat and looks at* **Harvey**; *a dead-eyed stare.*

Harvey   'Cause there's times I know you don't listen. I hope I'm not just talking to myself here?

Walter *stares at him.*

Harvey   What? What? What's that look for? What? You never do somethin' unpredictable? Well excuse me, Miss Perfect. You're flawless. I don't know whether to kiss your feet or nail you to a fuckin' tree. Look, I'm sorry I got you outta bed. But gimme a break, will ya? I'm explainin' myself here. Jesus Christ.

Harvey *continues and* **Walter** *begins sawing again, but he does not resume the hymn.*

Harvey   . . . So I'm standing there with my dick in my hand
pissing on a three-foot gnome. And it's good. *Yes*. Worth living
for. And then, then I take a look down and I realise . . . I see
what's happening. I'm pissing on a *leprechaun*. OK? The
gnome? The *thing*? Turns out a fuckin' leprechaun. It's true.
Bright green. Singing with his mouth open like this (*Stretches
open his mouth.*) and I'm pissin' on him. In his mouth. In his
little red painted mouth. BOOM! I think of St Patrick's Day.
BOOM! Those big proud barrel-chested bastards banging
their drums. Every eye in the crowd streaming, all goose bumps
and jubilation, crying out to Christ and his buddy the patron
saint of Ireland. Then, BAM! I'm offended. Back comes my
heritage. *Bam*. It hits me in the belly like a .38 slug. BAM! My
heritage. A true-blood second-generation mother-fucking
Irishman. And I'm there. I can hear those drums again. I'm
right there. I'm thinking of a hundred generations of suffering
and oppression; a race of people persecuted like the fuckin'
Jews and it comes to *this* . . . In the Land of the Brave, the
Home of the Free, a bright-green, three-foot-high singing
leprechaun, and I'm pissing on it. In its *mouth*. And I start to
feel the beginnings of *rage*. It's rising up in me like sick, like
fuckin' bile. I'm offended and *outraged* now. Who in the name
of sweet holy fuck would be so callous as to do such a thing?
To have this here? Who? I'm affronted. I'm angry. 'You racist
mother-fuckers! You racist fuckin' white-trash pig-suckin'
scum!' I'm screaming up at the windows now. Through no
fault of my own I'm pissing on a symbol of my ancestors. You
understand? *Our* ancestors. 'You racist fuckin' prick! You
white-trash piece of shit! Why don't you just come right out
and fuck me up the ass? Come on! Fuck me up the ass like you
did the home of my ancestors. Come on and fuck me, you
trashy piece of shit!' Then, then I glance over my shoulder . . .
and there's this guy standin' there. And get this: a postman. It's
true. A fuckin' *postman*? And all of a sudden . . . I'm *self-aware*.
I'm seeing what this guy's seeing: a bellicose drunk getting a
blow-job from a midget. A guy getting sucked off whilst
hurling abuse at the suckee. A midget dressed as a friggin'
leprechaun. And from his point of view I'm thinking that he

could construe this as some tramp in a suit being racially offensive to the Irish. Which was not in fact the fuckin' case. And this . . . it's the opposite . . . And this guy's just watchin' me. And in his face I see *disgust*. In his eyes I see disgust and *pity*. *PITY?!* A postman is pitying *me*? A fuckin' deadbeat, rainy-day *postman*? I get to where I am today walking in these shoes, and this guy is takin' time out of his petty little fuckin' life to pity *me*? Now my temper is going in another direction *entirely*. Now I'm thinking 'You self-righteous little shit. Ya little . . . You pond-life, you bottom-feeder, ya fuckin' troglodyte!' So I turn to him and look him in the eye: 'Fuck you lookin' at, asshole? Wanna piece of this, huh? Want me to blow you away?' Then, *self-awareness* hits me again and I realise that I'm sayin' these words to him with my *dick* in my hand. And he sees this. An' ya know? Ya know what the cocksucker does now? He starts to laugh. Tha' fuck. And I know by the sound of that laugh that he's *German*. I just *know it*. An' you know how I hate the Germans? Especially one in a uniform. And he sees quite fucking clearly the change in me now and he stops laughin'. *Yes.* Even though my Johnny Thomas is hangin' out danglin' like a fat fish and there's piss all down my trouser leg, he's stopped laughing. *Yes.* He's not laughin' any more. *No.* No more shall that Nazi supercilious fuck laugh at a decent man caught in the moment of a small indiscretion. (*A small, sudden violence.*) BAM! Pops 'im clean through the forehead. Drops like a side of beef. BUMPF. His face is gone. BAM! One more in his fat ass just for good measure. BAM! I shoot the leprechaun, put my piece back in my pants, put my dick back in my johns and take a leisurely stroll over to the call box. Dial your number like I'm in a dream. I tell ya, I felt better. I released something. And it wasn't just a bladder full of piss. I felt different. Better. Elevated . . . Something . . . ya know? I did the world a couple of favours in the space of a few heartbeats and I didn't get paid a fucking *dime*.

Pause.

Harvey   Huh?

He lifts a bundle at his feet: a large pair of shoes upon a crumpled blue uniform and a postman's mail sack. He goes to the furnace and throws them into the flames.

Free will. *Yes.* That's what that is. Yes. *Free will.* It's not all about money. Sometimes . . . sometimes you just gotta do what you think is right.

Beat.

I'm hungry.

Blackout.

Music: 'Bad Moon Rising' by Creedence Clearwater Revival.

Act One

Scene One

The Shamrock bar.

Late morning. A Brooklyn Irish bar. The men occupy this space as if it's their own. For the moment there is no drink being taken. There is a palpable restless male energy in the room.

'Bad Moon Rising' continues to play on a jukebox at the end of the bar. **Rourke** *dances in front of it.* **Wicklow** *and* **Antrim** *dance near him. As the music finishes,* **Rourke** *punches the jukebox and laughs.*

Rourke   Takin' it to the church!

Wicklow   I'm outta breath.

Rourke   Love that fuckin' song.

Antrim   It's good.

Rourke   We're goin' to the fuckin' moon!

Antrim   It's a good song.

Rourke   I'm gonna play it again.

O'Hare   No. I'm sick listening to it.

Rourke   C'mon. 'S great tune.

O'Hare   Not after the third time.

Rourke   C'mon, Mary.

O'Hare   Don't call me that.

Rourke   What's a matter?

O'Hare   I'm fuckin' serious.

Rourke   Keep your hair on.

Wicklow *begins to sing.* **Rourke** *and* **Antrim** *join in.*

Wicklow
Oh sugar, sugar, do do do do do do
Oh honey, honey, do do do do do do
You are my candy girl,
And you got me wanting you . . .

Rourke   Who sings that one?

Wicklow   Fuck knows. Good tune though.

O'Hare   What time you got?

Rourke   Quarter past.

O'Hare   What time he say he'd be here?

Rourke   Fifteen minutes ago.

O'Hare   Should we be worried?

Rourke   Probably just runnin' late.

O'Hare   What do ya call that stuff, anyways?

Rourke   What?

O'Hare   That fuckin' stuff on the ceiling?

Rourke   Blood?

O'Hare   Nah. That twirly shit up there?

Rourke   Where?

O'Hare   Round the light. The swirls and stuff?

Rourke   The decorative stuff?

O'Hare   Yeah.

Lumpy   Filigree.

They all look at **Tom 'Lumpy' Flannegan**, *who is eating a foot-long hotdog.*

Rourke   Guy's a regular thesaurus.

O'Hare   A what?

Rourke   Thesaurus.

O'Hare   Fuck's that?

Rourke   It's Greek.

Wicklow   Fuckin' Greeks.

Rourke   Means 'house of words'.

Wicklow   Faggots.

Rourke   Guy's a house of words.

Wicklow   Guy's a house.

Lumpy   Filigree. Definition: 'ornamental art'.

Rourke   See?

Lumpy   Synonyms: fretwork, lattice, interlace, arabesque, braid, curlicue, finery, frill, frippery, furbelow, garniture, gewgaws, gilt, spangle, tinsel, trinket . . . wreath.

Beat.

Antrim   Fuck.

Wicklow   Curly-cue?

Rourke   Impressive, ain't he?

O'Hare   Still doesn't tell me what that is?

Rourke   He just said.

O'Hare   He said a lotta stuff.

Rourke   And it all means pretty much the same thing. Don't it, Lumpy?

Lumpy   Kinda.

O'Hare   Where'd you learn all them words anyways?

Lumpy   *Reader's Digest.*

Rourke   I'm thirsty.

O'Hare   Must have a good memory.

Wicklow   Stores it in his fat.

Rourke   Ignore 'im, Tommy.

O'Hare   Fili . . . filla – what the fuck is it?

Lumpy   Filigree.

O'Hare   OK.

Lumpy   My favourite word? Lately?

Antrim   I can remember the day I was born.

Wicklow   Crap.

Lumpy   'Fulminate'.

Wicklow (*generally, indicating* **Antrim**)   Yous hear what this guy just said?

Lumpy (*speaking through the following dialogue*)   'Fulminate'. Definition: criticise harshly. Synonyms: berate, castigate, declaim, denounce, rage, rail, reprobate, thunder . . . vituperate.

Wicklow   Says he can remember bein' born.

Antrim   Like it was yesterday.

Wicklow   You can't remember two minutes ago.

Antrim   I remember plenty.

Wicklow   Go shit yourself a new brain.

O'Hare   An' that all means the same as, the same as the word that you said?

Lumpy   Fulminate. They relate to it, yeah. They're synonyms.

O'Hare   Cinnamons?

Lumpy   Synonyms. Means 'synonymous with'. Alternatives.

Antrim (*quietly*)   Syn – on – yms.

Rourke   I need a drink.

O'Hare   Fuck me. That's crazy.

Wicklow   What is?

O'Hare   As if there aren't enough fuckin' words in the world as it is an' then along comes all these other words that mean the same thing?

Lumpy *nods.*

Rourke   Anybody seen Harve?

O'Hare   That's fuckin' crazy.

Wicklow   What's crazy?

O'Hare   All the fuckin' words in the world.

Wicklow   Does seem to be a lot of 'em, alright.

O'Hare   It's fucked-up.

Wicklow   How is it? Why?

O'Hare   As if it isn't hard enough as it is to understand people, ya know? As if it isn't hard enough already to know what the fuck some guys rabbitin' at ya, without all these other words complicatin' everything and everythin'. You know?

Rourke   Muddying the water, so to speak?

O'Hare   Yeah. Do we really need it?

Rourke   Muddying the water, an' all.

O'Hare   Do we really need all these, these, whadda ya call 'em?

Rourke   What?

O'Hare   These extra words.

Lumpy   Embellishments.

O'Hare   Huh?

Lumpy   Filigree. Verbal ornamentation. You're saying that all these extra words are just frills and frippery?

O'Hare   That's exactly what I'm saying. Frills and frippery. Do we really need 'em?

Rourke   I'm inclined to agree with ya, Marion.

O'Hare   Huh?

Rourke   I'm inclined to say 'fuck words'.

O'Hare   But you know what I mean?

Rourke   I do. I really do. Anybody seen Harvey?

Antrim   He's with Walter. On a job.

O'Hare   All these words.

Wicklow   Yeah.

O'Hare   There's too many of 'em. Fuckin' words?

Rourke   They just complicate things.

O'Hare   They do.

Rourke   Yeah, they complicate things.

O'Hare   Hard enough to communicate with people as it is.

Rourke   Complications an' all.

O'Hare   Money. Now that's language.

Wicklow   Fuckin' A.

O'Hare   That's a fuckin' language we all speak.

Rourke   That's the one.

O'Hare   That's the one makes it all go round.

Wicklow   Money.

O'Hare   That's the one.

Rourke   Dollars.

Wicklow   Bingo-bango. Gimme some of them.

O'Hare We earn it. Deserve it. And these fucks try and deprive us of it?

Antrim Who?

O'Hare Government. With all their government speech and politicians. I know. I deal with these fucks every day.

Rourke What?

O'Hare They don't talk straight. They don't walk on the narrow.

Wicklow Like 'law-speak'.

O'Hare Huh? Exactly.

Wicklow The way lawyers speak.

Rourke Assholes.

O'Hare Exactly.

Wicklow All shit they say.

Lumpy Babel.

O'Hare Huh?

Wicklow All the shit.

O'Hare Why can't they just speak fuckin' English?

Rourke Fuck English.

O'Hare Why?

Rourke We don't speak English.

O'Hare No.

Lumpy Anglo-Irish American.

O'Hare Fuck is that?

Lumpy What we're speakin' now. Isn't that right, Johnny?

Rourke Speakin' straight. Speakin' true.

Wicklow Lawyers is the opposite.

O'Hare   They use that wise-guy talk to confuse the man off the street.

Rourke   Assholes.

O'Hare   All of 'em . . .

Wicklow   'S like they're talkin' fuckin' Latin.

Rourke   Assholes.

O'Hare   'Blah-blah de-blah blah-blah.' What the fuck does that mean?

Antrim   Means: 'Fuck you, I got an education!'

Wicklow   Fuckin' lawyers.

O'Hare   A guy should talk straight.

Rourke   Fuckin' A.

O'Hare   A guy should say what he means.

Rourke   I agree.

O'Hare   Huh?

Rourke   Say what he means.

O'Hare   Hard enough as it is understanding people as it is.

Wicklow   Yeah. I shouldn't say this . . .

Rourke   What?

Wicklow   I shouldn't say it.

O'Hare   Go on. Say it.

Wicklow   I spoke to a guy straight off the boat, ya know, from back home?

Antrim   Ireland?

Wicklow   No. Fuckin' Poland.

Rourke   Whereabouts?

Wicklow   The fucking Republic of Cork.

Rourke   Jeeez. A Cork man?

Wicklow   Straight off of the fuckin' boat. Yesterday. I was doin' the Hudson shake.

Rourke   How'd that go, by the way?

Wicklow   Pretty good. So, he asks me for a light . . . I swear to God, God forgive me, I couldn't understand a fuckin' word.

Rourke   Yeah?

Wicklow   It was just noise. (*The musicality of a Cork accent.*) Waaww, waw-waw-waw-waawww!

Lumpy   Poor bastard.

Wicklow   It was just noise. Waaaw-waw-waw.

Antrim   They probably said the same of your folk.

Wicklow   What?

Antrim   When they washed up here.

Wicklow   Hey. We're Dubliners. Born and bred.

Antrim   Like I said.

Wicklow   Fuck you.

Lumpy   We created the 'new' English.

O'Hare   Huh?

Lumpy   American.

Rourke   That's right.

O'Hare   Huh?

Lumpy   'So long'. Know where that came from?

Rourke   Wait'll you hear about this.

O'Hare   What?

Rourke   This is great.

O'Hare   What?

Lumpy   'So long'? Comes from Irish Gaelic: '*Slan.*'

Beat.

O'Hare   Get outta here.

Rourke   John fuckin' Wayne. 'So long!'

Lumpy   *Slan.*

O'Hare   Jesus H. Christ. He's fuckin' right!

Lumpy   Sucker. You know where that comes from?

Antrim   What?

Lumpy   Slang word, 'sucker', comes from the Irish *sach ur.* Means 'fresh, well-fed fellow' or 'fat cat'.

Wicklow   Get the fuck?

Lumpy   'S true.

O'Hare   Who would a' thought.

Rourke   Crazy, huh?

O'Hare   I use that word all the time.

Antrim   Me too.

O'Hare   Every fuckin' day of my life.

Rourke   It's Irish.

O'Hare   I don't know about yous, but I'm feeling a small pang of pride here.

Rourke   Without even knowing it, you been speaking Irish all your goddam life.

Laughter.

O'Hare   All my life.

A noise outside and they all instantly look to the door. It opens and **Gulliver Sullivan** *walks in – a charismatic man who has aged well and dresses flawlessly. Those seated stand, except* **O'Hare**, *in deference to their boss. He motions for them to sit with a benevolent smile.*

Sullivan   Gentlemen, I apologise for the early meeting but we have important matters to discuss. But, before we conduct our business, I'm going to introduce you to someone. Now I want you to be civil and watch your language.

He motions to someone beyond the doorway. A sixteen-year-old boy enters in scruffy denims. He has unruly hair and big, serious, unfathomable eyes.

Sullivan   This is my nephew, Bobby.

They all mutter a greeting to the boy.

This sorry lot here are my employees. Come on in, Bobby, they won't bite.

The boy shuffles forwards.

This here is Antrim O'Malley. Don't shake his hands, Bobby. God knows where they've been. Greet him with your eyes, Daniel. Now there's a smile. That there is Billy Wicklow. Beside him is chief Marion O'Hare, NYPD.

O'Hare   Except I don't work for him, kid, we're business associates.

Sullivan   That's what I let him think.

Laughter. Not from **O'Hare**.

Sullivan   The big fella there is Tom Lumpy Flannagan, Jesus Mary and Joseph, Tommy. Is it my imagination or have you put on weight?

Lumpy   I have, Mr Sullivan.

O'Hare   Needs to eat more apples.

Lumpy   Apples?

O'Hare   They're a fruit. You eat 'em.

Sullivan   What's happening, Tom?

Lumpy   It's the sedentary lifestyle, Mr Sullivan.

Sullivan   It's the cakes, Lumpy. It's the *cakes*. And this? This reprobate is Johnny 'The Fox' Rourke. Bit of a ladies' man.

Rourke   I'm a magnet, Mr Sullivan. I can't help it.

Laughter.

Sullivan   You're a rogue.

Rourke   That I am.

Sullivan   Come see me afterwards, Johnny. Nice shoes. OK, fellas. Now listen up. Bobby here is over from Belfast. The old turf. Belfast, County Antrim. He had a little trouble there back home and his mom thought he might be better over here for a while. Maybe just for the summer until things cool down. And I want you to make him feel welcome. He's one of my family so treat him as such. But what am I doing? He's nearly a grown man he can speak for himself. Bobby?

Bobby *looks at* **Sullivan**.

Sullivan   Anything you'd like to say?

Bobby *looks at them all in silence. He shakes his head.*

Sullivan   Man of few words. I like that.

They laugh.

Sullivan   Man of few words.

Lumpy   Taciturn.

Sullivan   Hm?

Lumpy   Taciturn. Means 'man of few words'.

Sullivan   Yes.

Silence.

Sullivan   Welcome to Brooklyn, Bobby.

Blackout.

Scene Two

Sullivan's *place.*

Sullivan *sits behind a large antique desk, a black Bakelite telephone within easy reach.* **Rourke** *stands in front of the desk, grinning.*

Rourke   How much?

Sullivan   A hundred thousand.

Rourke   A hundred grand? In cash?

Sullivan   Hundred-dollar bills.

Rourke *whistles.*

Sullivan   Tax-free.

Rourke *looks at him.*

Sullivan   That was a joke.

Rourke *laughs, perhaps obediently.*

Sullivan   I talked to him last night. He called me.

Rourke   So he's buying a truce?

Sullivan   You could say that.

Rourke   Marconi's bowing down to you.

Sullivan   Let's not get too carried away. 'It's a token of our new understanding.' His words. We're not allies all of a sudden. We're not climbing into bed with the Italians. We are just agreeing to stop trying to kill each other. Marconi's getting old. I guess he's tired of looking over his shoulder. It's his wish to die peacefully in bed and with the knowledge that his sons will outlive him.

Rourke   When's he payin' up?

Sullivan   Today. Tomorrow. He'll send two of his men when he has the money together.

Rourke   OK.

Sullivan   Now listen to me, John. Are you listening?

Rourke   I am.

Sullivan   Until I say otherwise there is to be no further conflict with the Italians. I want the men to know this. For the foreseeable future we are now at peace with Marconi and his men. However unpalatable that may be. All grudges are forgotten. All debts are paid. If I accept this offering into my hands it is a bond and I will not on principle break that bond. My word is iron. Anyone who jeopardises this arrangement will pay severely. Anyone screws it up is history. *Anyone.* We can't afford a war with the Italians.

Rourke   We'd kick their ass.

Sullivan   There would be a high body count, yes, but they outnumber us four to one. No. To survive we have to adapt. Now, on pain of death this peace will be upheld. Do I make myself clear?

Rourke   Yes. Yes, Mr Sullivan.

Sullivan   Good. Tell the boys. Do not mention the money. You hear me? That's between you and me. But you tell them my orders. Marconi offered a truce. End of story. And be sure to tell Walter and Harvey. O'Keefe, Ryan and Joey too. No more yahoos. I want this ceasefire operational from the moment I finish this sentence.

Pause.

Rourke   Understood.

Sullivan   Good.

Pause. **Sullivan** *studies* **Rourke**.

Sullivan   How are you?

Rourke   Me? I'm good.

Sullivan   Yeah?

Rourke   Yeah. Couldn't be better.

Pause.

Sullivan   When was the last time you were in church?

Rourke   When was the last time? In church? I dunno. Richy's funeral?

Sullivan   I mean of your own free will.

Rourke   I dunno. A while?

Sullivan   You should go.

Rourke   Yeah?

Sullivan   Yes.

Rourke   OK then. I will.

Sullivan   Good.

Pause

How is sobriety?

Rourke   Good. Thinkin' straight. Thinkin' true.

Sullivan   Good.

Pause.

How are the guys?

Rourke   They're good.

Sullivan   No rumblings?

Rourke   Not that I can hear.

Sullivan   Good. Keep an ear out.

Rourke   Sure.

Pause.

Sullivan   I rely on you, Johnny. You're my left hand. I trust you. Don't disappoint me.

Rourke   I won't.

Sullivan   I know.

Blackout.

Scene Three

The Hudson River. Docks.

The deep, mournful wail of a foghorn. The sound of water lapping against concrete.

Lights up on:

Chief **Marion O'Hare**. *He is dressed in a large black police-issue coat, his hands buried deep in the pockets. He is singing 'Danny Boy' quietly to himself but he is not the best of singers and his heart isn't in it.*

Sullivan *approaches silently behind him.*

Sullivan   You're scaring the fish.

O'Hare *starts.*

O'Hare   Jesus. I didn't hear you comin'. You alone?

Sullivan   What's the rumpus?

O'Hare   All this shit with the moon. City's gone crazy. I mean, why the fuck would anyone wanna go up there in the first place? It's crazy. You gonna watch it?

Sullivan   I'm busy.

O'Hare   I gotta. The boys wanna watch it. Wife bought a new TV set. Month's fuckin' wages.

Sullivan   Why am I here?

Beat.

O'Hare   Couple a' things.

Sullivan   Shoot.

O'Hare   Hennessey.

Sullivan   Jim Hennessey? What about him?

O'Hare   He's mouthin' off.

Sullivan   What's he saying?

O'Hare   I'm embarrassed to tell ya.

Sullivan   Tell me.

O'Hare   He's an asshole. He's getting real cocky.

Beat.

He's saying things. In public, ya know?

Sullivan   No. I don't know. Tell me.

O'Hare   I dunno, Gulliver.

Beat.

Sullivan   Speak.

Beat.

O'Hare   He's sayin' you're on the way out. Can you believe this? He has the balls to say this. He says the Italians are takin' over and the Irish are on their way out. He said . . . an' this is in Joe's Bar, ya know, full a' cops, he says this in front of everyone, he says, and forgive me for sayin' this 'cause it's unkind and untrue. He says 'Sully's an old-school muck-savage. A ditch-digging immigrant. He hasn't got the balls or know-how any more to stand up to the Italians.'

Pause.

Sullivan   Go on.

O'Hare   He says the Irish gangs is over. He said 'Sullivan's a dinosaur and I ain't paying another fuckin' dime to 'im.' That's what he said. Thereabouts. Didn't say it to me but I was there. He was speakin' loud. I heard some of it, so I swear on my fuckin' life, that's what he said.

Sullivan   You didn't hear all of it?

O'Hare   Not all of it, but I heard what I had to hear.

Pause.

Sullivan   Who was he talking to?

O'Hare   He was talkin' loud.

Sullivan   Who?

O'Hare   Couple of guys I didn't recognise. And another guy was one of Marconi's.

Sullivan   Marconi. You're sure about this?

O'Hare   Yeah. Name's Manfreedee or somethin'. I dunno, they all sound like dishes off of a menu to me.

Beat.

I hate being the bearer of bad tidings an' all that.

Beat.

I just thought you should know.

Pause.

Sullivan   You and Hennessey have never been the best of friends.

O'Hare   I hate him, the lippy fuck. But what of that?

Pause.

Sullivan   What's the other thing?

O'Hare   Huh?

Sullivan   You said 'a couple of things'.

O'Hare   Yeah.

Beat.

Sullivan   Well?

O'Hare   Harvey.

Beat.

Harvey Marr.

Beat.

A fuckin' postman?

Beat.

What's that about?

Beat.

Guy's off his nuts. I mean a *postman*? How am I gonna explain this away? It isn't easy. Makes things difficult. Sorrow's good. He's good at his job. In, out, everything clean, but people ask questions. A junkie or a black kid maybe, but a postman? Poor bastard's only probably goin' about his business. People like postmen. Postmen are people.

Sullivan   Now he's cinders. Anybody report him missing?

O'Hare   Not yet.

Sullivan   A lonely guy.

O'Hare   We don't know.

Sullivan   Witnesses?

O'Hare   Nobody come forward yet. Nobody's sayin' anything, but that doesn't mean they didn't see anything.

Pause.

Sullivan   Let's play it by ear. It'll go away.

O'Hare   If it doesn't?

Sullivan   Make something up.

O'Hare   Like what?

Beat.

Sullivan   He was pushing drugs on his post round. A local gang whacked him. End of story.

O'Hare   And Harvey?

Sullivan   Leave him to me.

O'Hare   He's a loose cannon.

Sullivan   He had a bad day.

O'Hare He's a liability.

Beat.

Sullivan Don't make me explain myself to you.

Pause.

Sullivan *produces a thick brown envelope and passes it to* **O'Hare**.

Sullivan Go buy your wife a hat.

O'Hare *weighs the envelope in his hand.*

O'Hare This all?

Sullivan Don't get greedy, O'Hare. It's a deadly sin.

O'Hare *puts the envelope into his coat pocket. He pauses as if to say something, then thinks better of it and leaves. For a moment* **Sullivan** *is left standing alone.*

Wicklow *appears silently from the shadows and arrives at his side.*

Sullivan Prospect Heights. 589 Vanderbilt Avenue. He lives alone. Use your feet.

Beat.

Wicklow He have a name?

Sullivan Hennessey.

Blackout.

Scene Four

A tenement rooftop garden. Night.

The muted sounds of the city: the low hum of traffic, car horns, the distant wail of police sirens.

Lights up slow to reveal a rooftop garden, tenderly cared for.

Sullivan *and* **Bobby** *stand looking out and up at a full moon.*

Sullivan   'We choose to go to the moon in this decade and do the other things, not because they are easy but because they are hard.' An Irishman said that eight years ago in the state of Texas. His name was John F. Kennedy and he was president of the greatest country in the world. A true pioneer. From Ireland, to America, to the moon. That's quite a journey. I thought him a great man. Others disagreed. They put a bullet in his head and sent him to God.

Pause.

There will come a day, Bobby, when God will judge me. It'll be swift as I imagine there will be quite a queue. And in those brief moments of appraisal, in those seconds of recognition, I believe my Lord God will see necessity in my actions. I believe that he will say *'This man did what he had to do.'* God forbid I become a man who is haunted by his actions. No. My conscience is clear. I have done and will continue to do what has to be done. I'm not a good man, I'm not a bad man neither. I'm not a genius, but I'm not stupid. But I'm true to my word. My word is iron. And I act as the situation requires me to.

Silence.

They continue to look out . . .

This city is changing. Different world from when I was a boy. You know what getting old is? Getting old is slowly losing everything that you're familiar with.

Silence.

He suddenly stamps his foot. It makes a dull thud.

You hear that?

He stamps his foot again.

Try it.

The strangeness of this request makes **Bobby** *smile self-consciously.*

Sullivan   Go on.

Bobby *tentatively stamps his foot.*

Sullivan   Again. Harder.

Bobby *stamps his foot harder.*

Sullivan   Feels good, doesn't it? You know why? Under your feet? That's turf from Kildare. Horse country. There's an energy in it. I had it shipped over from home. Little bit of home. These trees? Apple tree from County Armagh. Apple country. Ecclesiastical capital of Ireland. Ash tree from Fermanagh. That's a blackthorn from Letterkenny, County Donegal. That's a sapling oak from County Cavan. Don't know where that is, but it's somewhere in the middle. Lavender from County Clare. Put this under your pillow, helps you sleep. Laurel tree from Hillsborough, County Down. Nasturtiums from a window box in Derry City. The walled city. This is my little bit of home. My little piece of Eden. This is home.

They look out into the night.

Sullivan   You know what Ireland is, Bobby?

Bobby *looks up at* **Sullivan** *with an unreadable expression and after a moment slowly shakes his head.*

Sullivan   Ireland is where the wind blows it.

Pause.

You miss it?

A small nod from **Bobby**.

Sullivan   You leave Ireland, Bobby, you never really leave it. It's always there. It's like the moon. Always with you, even when you can't see it. It's like it's got a pull on you. I know a lot of men here who pine for it and they've never even been there.

Pause.

You cold?

Bobby *shakes his head.*

Sullivan   You want my jacket?

Bobby *shakes his head.*

Sullivan   C'mon. Take my jacket.

He takes off his jacket and drapes it around **Bobby***'s thin shoulders.*

Sullivan   There you go. That's better. We gotta feed you up.

Pause.

Don't lie to your family, Bobby. Blood. Honour your blood. Be true to it. You do something wrong, somethin' keeps you awake at night, somethin' makes your brain go gurgle? You go to the church and you confess. Not everything. Sometimes you have to be economical with the truth, for your sake and whoever it is that's listening. But you sit there and you dump it in the confession box. That's what it's there for. It's a laundromat. The Irish American Catholic's laundromat of the soul. That's what it's for. I'm not criticising it. I value it. It's the rock upon which I have built my life. Without the church the Irish would be a defeated people long ago. It gave us succour when we suffered. The Irish race have suffered. Maybe more even than the Jews. They teach you about the famine back home?

Bobby *nods.*

Sullivan   Then you know what I'm talking about. A nation of exiles. Adversity. But we are a resilient people and I have come to believe that in exile a man finds his true nature. Look at what we have achieved. We built this country with our bare hands. Nearly broke our backs doing it. Once we were thought of no better than slaves. They called us pale Indians. White Negros. Now they call us Governor, Senator, President. How about that? Sixteen presidents of Irish descent. We number half the NYPD and we practically founded the FBI. 'S true. The Irish made America. Then all the others started pouring in. But enough of that. What I'm saying, Bobby, is . . . you're home. And don't let anyone ever disrespect you because of your heritage. You pop 'em in the kisser and then remind them that America is what it is today because of an exodus from the

old country a hundred years ago. They disrespect you again?
You put 'em down for good. Sometimes, words are not
enough. You hear me, Bobby? You hear what I'm telling you?

Bobby *nods.*

Sullivan   And always keep your shoes clean. Good shoes are
important. We are who we are from the ground up.

Pause.

Your mother ever talk about me? She ever tell you what I do?

Bobby *looks at him.*

Sullivan   I am a peacekeeper, of a kind. I'm a business man
first but I also keep the peace. Ten blocks that way and about
twenty blocks that way. That's a lot a' ground. I have men who
work for me, some of whom you have met, and they help me
do what I have to do. Some of them are policemen, some civil
servants, some of them straight off the boat, and some of
them are politicians. Yes, even politicians. They come to me
because, like I said, sometimes words are not enough. I do
what the police and the politicians can't or won't be seen to be
doing. I do the unseen. I just try to keep things running
smoothly. It ain't easy. The nature of man dictates that things
never always run according to plan. There's always a kink.
Always a bubble that needs smoothed out. What's needed is an
iron hand. And that I provide. A civic duty. And I profit from it.

Pause.

*He takes out his wallet and opens it. It is thick with money. He takes a
twenty-dollar bill from the wallet and holds it out to* **Bobby**.

Sullivan   This is the only money I'm ever going to give you,
Bobby. The rest . . . you have to earn.

Bobby *looks at the money.*

Sullivan   Go on, take it.

Bobby *takes the money.*

Sullivan   The world can be an ugly place, Bobby. Man's nature makes it so. You're nearly a man, so the sooner you learn that the better. I know that you came from a troubled place. You saw things. You'll see things here . . . But hear and believe this: all that I do is for the greater good. You hear me? I seek the *light*, Bobby, for in *darkness* we dwindle.

They look out together for a moment, up at the moon.

Hey.

Bobby *looks at him.*

Sullivan   You wanna steak?

Bobby *smiles briefly.*

Blackout.

Act Two

Scene One

An apartment. Prospect Heights. Day.

Darkness.

Heavy breathing. Muttered curses. The unseen labours of several men. The sound of something being kicked repeatedly.

Another sound: becoming discernible, the reverential tones of a news commentator reporting live on the Apollo 11 moon landing.

Lights up slow on **Rourke** *and* **Bobby**. *They sit on a threadbare sofa downstage right in front of a television perched on a wooden stool. The flickering light from the TV screen illuminates* **Rourke**'s *face: intense concentration, a barely contained, childlike excitement.*

Bobby *is beside him. Only the back of his head is visible. He is looking over the back of the sofa, upstage into the darkness. He seems captivated, riveted by the spectacle of what we can hear but cannot yet see.*

The quiet sound of kicking continues through the following. **Rourke** *does not take his eyes from the screen.*

Rourke   Jesus . . .

Beat.

Jesus Christ . . .

Beat.

Jesus H. Christ . . .

Pause.

Shit me . . . You see this, Bobby? This is history. Right here. Right now. This is huge. You'll remember this. Mark my words. Like the day they shot Kennedy. Forty years from now you'll remember where you were when man first set foot on the moon. With your Uncle Johnny. Man's gonna walk on the *moon*. Can you believe it? Man's gonna walk on the moon and we're gonna *watch* him! I can't decide which is crazier. We're goin' to another world. Buck Rogers. Captain fuckin' Kirk. After this? Mark my words, Bobby, after this, nothing will be the same again. The world changes from this day on. From here on in. This is the greatest moment in the history of, of, of man! Soon as he steps out up there . . . Boom! Man loses his virginity. That's kinda what it is. We're about to lose our cosmic virginity. (*Grinning.*) How about that? You know how many people are watching this? Three billion. Around the world. That's half the population of the planet. This is history. You wanna know something funny? Man flying the Command Module? The little ship circlin' the moon's gonna bring those guys back home? Know what his name is? Nobody else seems to have picked up on this but it doesn't escape me. I notice these things. The man flyin' the Command Module is called, get this, Michael Collins. (*Laughs.*) How about that? An Irish revolutionary in space. Flyin' round the moon! Mike Collins. Stranger than fiction. They gotta be related.

In a sudden explosion of irritation **Rourke** *glances back into the darkness.*

He snaps back to the TV as lights come up slow upstage and discover what is holding **Bobby**'s *attention.*

Three men are revealed darkly. They surround the prone shape of a curled-up body, a lifeless thing animated in jolts by their kicking feet. They go about this methodically, with no sense of passion, only a slow, steady dedication to their work.

Rourke   Guys! Fuck me!

Wicklow   What?

Rourke   We're watching this here!

Wicklow   Well, we're workin' over here.

Rourke   Keep the noise down, can't ya?

Antrim   This is business.

Rourke   Why can't you use a bullet like any other decent human being?

He returns to the TV.

Assholes. Bobby, don't look at that, look at this.

Bobby *looks briefly at the TV, but in moments his attention returns to the action upstage.*

Lumpy *stops kicking and steps back from the others, clutching his right arm. He has a half-eaten hotdog in one hand. The others stop.*

Wicklow   Whatcha doin'?

Lumpy   My arm hurts.

Wicklow   You unfit fat fuck. (*To* **Antrim**.) His arm hurts.

Antrim   Fuck his arm. My feet hurt. Isn't he dead yet?

Wicklow   Oh yeah. He's dead ages ago.

Antrim   Then why are we still kickin' 'im, then?

Wicklow   Mr Sullivan wants him to suffer.

Lumpy   Well, he's double dead so let's call it quits.

Wicklow   What, are we keepin' you from your food?

Lumpy   My arm hurts.

Wicklow   Probably havin' a heart attack, you fat fuck.

Antrim *laughs.*

Lumpy   Stop callin' me that.

Wicklow *laughs.*

Lumpy   I'm serious! You're giving me a complex.

Wicklow   I'll give you complex right up your big fat ass, you bucket of blubber.

Antrim *suddenly looks down at the body.*

Antrim   You hear that?

Wicklow   What?

Antrim   He made a noise.

Lumpy   Him?

Antrim   Yeah.

Wicklow   Probably air escaping.

Antrim   No.

Wicklow   Punctured lung.

Antrim   No, it came from his face.

Wicklow   You sure?

Antrim   Yeah. Where his face should be.

Wicklow   Did he say something?

Antrim   Yeah. Maybe.

Lumpy   What he say?

Antrim   How the fuck should I know?

Wicklow   Listen and see if he's breathing.

Antrim   I ain't getting down in that shit.

Wicklow   C'mon, you're already bloody.

Antrim   Only my feet.

Wicklow   You're the one heard him.

Antrim   Maybe I imagined it.

Wicklow   Do it.

Antrim   Fuck.

Antrim *gets down and listens.*

Wicklow   Well?

Antrim   Shhh!

Rourke *glares at the TV.*

Rourke   What is that? Is that something? Is somethin'
happening? (*Beat.*) I wish something would happen. (*Beat.*) The
moon. Can you imagine it? Walking on the moon. Pure white.
No air. No sound. No cars. No garbage. No blood. Least not
yet anyways. Pure as virgin snow. Like the Antarctic. Only in
space. (*Beat.*) The space age they're callin' it. In our lifetime.
And it all starts here. It's a good time to be alive, Bobby.

Antrim *stands.*

Wicklow   Well?

Antrim   He's still breathing.

Wicklow   Fuck.

Antrim   Tough old bird, I'll give 'im that.

Lumpy   What do we do now?

Wicklow   We finish the job.

Antrim   With our feet?

Wicklow   Unless you wanna spoil your manicure? C'mon,
you fuckin' micks.

Resigned, they begin to kick the dying man again.

Rourke   It's happening! Something's happening. What is
that? It's all fuzzy and shit. I can't make that out, can you?
Bobby, what is it? Is that the side of the space ship or
somethin'? Is that what it is? All I can see is white. This
picture's fuckin' terrible. People pay taxes for this? Picture's
fuckin' – What is that?! Well, it's movin' whatever it is. Looks
like a big fuckin' marshmallow. Is that a man? Is that –

He calls over his shoulder.

It's a man! It's a man! Guys! Guys! They're doin' it! They're
about to do it! Watch this, Bobby. You'll be tellin' your
grandchildren about this some day. Listen . . .

The TV crackles and the sound fades out.

Hennessey, you cheap piece of shit.

He swiftly thumps the side of the TV and the sound crackles back.

Armstrong (*voice-over*)   . . . OK . . . I'm about to step off the ladder . . .

Rourke   Holy shit! Here we go! He's steppin' off! (*Warning the TV.*) Don't make me hit you again. Guys! He's stepping off the ladder! Keep it down! He's about to do it!

Beat.

Armstrong (*voice-over*)   . . . leap for mankind.

Pause.

Rourke   What'd he say?

Pause.

Rourke   Was that it? Leap for mankind? A leap? Jesus Christ. And that's it? Did we miss something? Christ. He must a' said somethin' before that and we missed it. We missed it! (*Over his shoulder.*) You selfish cocksuckers! What did he say, Bobby? Did you hear?

Bobby *shakes his head.*

Rourke   'Leap for mankind'. Underselling it a little, ain't he? A leap? Greatest moment in history? A leap? We must a' missed it. Shit.

The other three amble over with a box of tissues. They stop around the back of the sofa and begin wiping blood from their shoes with the tissues. **Rourke** *continues watching the TV.* **Bobby** *continues to stare at the dead man.*

Lumpy   They do it?

Rourke   Yeah.

Lumpy   What they say?

Rourke   Leap for mankind.

Wicklow   Huh?

Rourke   He said 'Leap for mankind'.

Lumpy   Is that it?

Rourke   It's all I caught. He probably said something before that but I couldn't hear it over your fuckin' shenanigans.

Wicklow   That was business.

Rourke   It was barbaric.

Wicklow   Sullivan wanted him to suffer.

Rourke   Barbaric. And why couldn't you make him suffer in the next room?

Beat.

Antrim   It's got a carpet.

Rourke (*mimicking*)   'It's got a carpet'. You think he cares any more? Ya prick. We gotta friggin' kid sittin' here. No offence, kid. You're givin' him the wrong impression. We're not savages.

Lumpy   Sorry, kid.

Antrim   Yeah, Bobby. Sorry.

Rourke   You wanna apologise to him for spoiling his enjoyment of the greatest moment in human fuckin' history.

Wicklow   What was that?

Rourke   A man just walked on to the moon, you shithead.

Wicklow   Nothin' to do with me.

Rourke   Fuckin' baboon.

Wicklow   Well, business is business. And you should a' been doin' your bit, Johnny.

Rourke   In hundred-dollar shoes?

Wicklow   Should of worn boots.

Rourke   Boots? With this suit?

Wicklow   Stop bein' a fag.

Rourke   Fuck you. Bunch of baboons.

Wicklow   We're professionals.

Rourke   Hooligans, the lot of ya. Ignore them, Bobby. Savages. No sense of propriety. You follow my lead. Man needs a sense of propriety.

Bobby *is looking at him now, ashen-faced.*

Rourke   You OK, kid?

Bobby *suddenly lurches forward and vomits on **Rourke**'s feet.*

Pause.

Rourke *looks up at the three men while **Bobby** recovers.*

Rourke   Now look what you did?

Bobby *stands unsteadily and leaves.*

Rourke   You'll be OK, Bobby. Happens first time to everyone.

Antrim   Yeah, Bob. Happened to me.

Bobby *has gone.*

Rourke   Hundred-dollar shoes. Gimme those fuckin' tissues.

Blackout.

Scene Two

Tenement rooftop garden.

Sullivan   How's the boy?

Rourke   Bobby? He's good. He's good.

Sullivan   You're showing him the ropes?

Rourke   Yeah.

Sullivan   You're looking out for him?

Rourke   Like he was my own brother.

Sullivan   You make sure he eats.

Rourke   I'll take him for a burger.

Sullivan   Get him a milkshake. A cheeseburger. Kid needs calcium. He's got to grow.

Rourke   Cheeseburger it is.

Sullivan   It's early days but I'd like to see him stay on a while.

Rourke   Yeah?

Sullivan   I like having him around.

Rourke   He seems like a nice kid.

Sullivan   It's nice having family around.

Rourke   Funny, I don't remember you ever telling me you had a sister?

Sullivan   I didn't.

Beat.

Who knows? He might even want to come into the business. You know, he's the image of my mother.

Rourke   Yeah? He looks a little like you.

Sullivan   You think?

Rourke   Yeah. Round the eyes.

Pause.

Sullivan   He say anything to you?

Rourke   Like what?

Sullivan   Has he spoken to you?

Rourke   No. He's quiet as a mouse.

Sullivan   I think he has intelligence. You can see it in his eyes. He watches. He listens.

Rourke   What happened to him, back home?

Sullivan   His mother thinks he's probably better off here. And I'm inclined to agree. Lot of trouble kicking off over there.

Rourke   Same as it ever was.

Pause.

Sullivan   You talk to Harvey?

Rourke   Yeah.

Sullivan   How is the old dog?

Rourke   Sheepish.

Sullivan   He sober?

Rourke   Pretty much.

Sullivan   I can't talk to him when he's drinking. He has to understand that.

Rourke   I think he does.

Sullivan   We all have our cross to bear, John. Harvey's is a bottle of bourbon. Mine seems to be Harvey, but I can't keep turning a blind eye every time he goes on a rampage. Makes me look weak.

Rourke   It'll blow over.

Sullivan   Send him up.

Rourke *leaves.* **Sullivan** *is left alone. Distantly we hear men's laughter. Then, softly,* **Harvey** *begins to sing 'The Auld Triangle'. He enters upstage and approaches* **Sullivan** *slowly, singing. He arrives at* **Sullivan***'s side and after a beat* **Sullivan** *joins him in the song. He sings the harmony, gently, restrained. They finish the song and continue to look out in silence.*

Harvey   How are you, ya little bastard?

Sullivan   I've been better.

Harvey   You and me both.

Sullivan   I haven't seen much of you.

Harvey   I been busy. You know, this and that.

Sullivan   How's your daughter?

Harvey   She's clean. Pretty much.

Sullivan   And . . . . . .

Harvey   Maggie? Oh, she's her grandaddy's little girl alright. Real fiery. She'll do OK. You know, I seen more of her growing up than my own daughter. I gave her a little doll an' all, ya know? Candy and shit.

Sullivan   You're doing OK by them.

Harvey   Yeah, well . . . some things you just can't fix.

Sullivan   You did good by me, Harvey. You looked out for me. I owe you.

Harvey   You don't owe me nothin'.

Sullivan   I do and it's said.

Pause.

Harvey   Is that an oak leaf?

Sullivan   Five years old, from County Cavan.

Harvey   Cavan, huh? Right in the middle. Your nasturtiums are looking good.

Sullivan   Well, they'll grow anywhere.

Harvey   They look good.

Beat.

Ya can eat 'em, ya know? . . . Like in a salad. They're peppery. Nutritious.

Sullivan   I didn't know that.

Pause.

Harvey   I fucked up.

Beat.

I fucked up. I was drinkin' bourbon. My brain was on fire. But it'll never happen again. This is the last time. As true as I'm standing here. This is me. Never again.

Pause.

Sullivan   OK then.

Harvey   OK then . . .

Pause.

Harvey   Walter's downstairs. He's singin' 'Onward Christian Soldiers' to Bobby. Kid's lookin' at him like he's a talkin' mushroom. What you gonna do with him? Bobby. Ya gonna keep him on?

Sullivan   Maybe.

Harvey   You sure about that?

Sullivan *looks at* **Harvey**.

Sullivan   I want you to observe this truce with the Italians. You break it . . . I can't protect you. I mean it.

He means it.

Harvey   I let you down, I'll put a cap in my head myself.

Pause.

Oh yeah, I got you somethin'.

He produces a small paper packet and offers it to **Sullivan**.

Harvey   Take it. It's a gift.

Sullivan *takes the packet and opens it, watched by* **Harvey**.

Harvey   It's real gold. It's a tiepin. You put it on your tie. It's Cuchulain. You know? The greatest Irish warrior . . . You better like it. Pawned a medal for it.

Sullivan   You shouldn't have done that.

Harvey   Well I did and it's done. What, you don't like it?

Sullivan   I do. Thank you, Harvey.

Harvey   Ah, don't be gettin' all mushy on me. Here, let me fix it for ya.

He puts it on **Sullivan***'s tie.*

Harvey   There ya go.

Sullivan   How do I look?

Harvey   Like a million dollars.

The moment is held while offstage, eight voices sing in perfect harmony:

'All around the banks of the Royal Canal
All around the banks of the Royal Canal.'

Scene Three

A diner.

Rourke *and* **Bobby** *sit opposite each other in a diner booth. Red leather seats and red-and-white checked plastic tablecloth. They are contained by a kind of sixties Formica nostalgia. A hooded red lamp illuminates their small table.*

Rourke   We watched the moon landing today in my mom's place. OK? She's a nice old lady. Wears a hair net and curlers an' all. Says she was born with her hair too straight. Donegal woman. She liked you.

Pause.

We watched the moon landing at my mom's place. In fact, tell you what, she gave us both a piece of her famous pumpkin pie. How about that? Wasn't it delicious?

Bobby *is staring out the window.*

Rourke   Hey. Bobby, you gotta look at me here.

Bobby *looks at him.*

Rourke   That's better. OK, so we were at my mom's today. She made us pie. She made us tea. Good old-fashioned God-honest Irish tea.

Pause.

What I'm saying . . . I'm just saying we don't need to tell your uncle about . . . you know? Might upset him. Let's just keep it to ourselves. It's not lying. It's . . . an omission. Something left out. Like garbage. Somethin' you leave out then forget about.

Pause.

Bobby, you gotta talk to me here. You're lookin' at me with those big serious eyes. You're doing intensity. I knew a lotta guys did intensity. They're all dead.

Beat.

Seriously though, you gotta open up a little. The silent thing gets a little creepy after a while to be honest with ya.

They study one another in silence. Nothing from **Bobby**.

Rourke   What? You're lookin' questions at me, might as well speak 'em.

Pause. Nothing from **Bobby**.

Rourke   How's your stomach?

Bobby *looks at him.*

Rourke   You wanna eat?

Bobby *nods.* **Rourke** *rises.*

Rourke   What you want? Cheeseburger and fries, milkshake?

Bobby *nods.*

Rourke   Back in a minute.

Rourke *leaves to order.* **Bobby** *is left alone. He picks up the salt shaker. Sets it down. He opens his mouth and closes it. He continues to do this perhaps to amuse himself. He then takes out the crumpled twenty-dollar bill* **Sullivan** *gave him and flattens it neatly on the tabletop. He holds the bill up to the light and mouths the words written there: 'In God We Trust'. He folds the money and puts it back in his pocket.*

Rourke *returns to the booth with two burgers, fries and Cokes.*

Rourke   Here ya go. Cheeseburgers.

He shares out the portions. He takes a quarter of whiskey out of his pocket and empties half into his own measure of Coke, then begins eating his burger. **Bobby** *watches him. When* **Rourke** *catches his eye he looks out the window. This continues for several moments in silence.*

Rourke   What?

Bobby *shrugs.*

Rourke   Aren't you gonna touch your food?

Bobby *nods.*

Rourke   I been comin' here for years. Coffee's good. Always been good. Puts hairs on your tongue. These burgers just slide down. Gotta warn you though, they slide outta ya too.

Pause.

Bobby   Mr Rourke?

Rourke *freezes halfway through a bite of his burger.*

Rourke   Bobby?

Bobby   That man. Who was he?

Beat.

Rourke   He was . . . He was just a guy.

Bobby   What did he do?

Rourke   What did he do? Oh he was . . . He was a bad man. He was stealing money off of your uncle Gulliver. Bad mouthing him, you know? Disrespecting him to others behind his back. He was a bad mouth and a thief.

Bobby *picks at his fries.*

Rourke   I don't know if Mr Sullivan has explained this to you, but on the streets here we live by a code. Ya know? You stay by the code. Everybody knows that. You go outside of the code and shit all over it and where's the code any more? Ya know? Where do we go then? Flaunting rules, willy-nilly, soon there's gonna be anarchy. You need structure. A sense of propriety. You need rules. A code. Even chaos has friggin' rules. You don't need a fancy education to work that out. *The National Geographic*. Worth a read. That guy? He flaunted the rules. He deserves to be dead. I'm sorry though, Bob. I'm sorry if it upset ya. I am. You didn't have to see that.

Bobby   See what? We were at your mum's place.

Rourke *looks at* **Bobby**. **Bobby** *holds the look.* **Rourke** *nods.*

Rourke   Yes, we were.

They eat.

Bobby   You think they're still up there?

Rourke   Who? The astronauts? Nah. They only got so much oxygen to last or some such thing. No, they're on their way back home. They planted a flag. They're comin' home. Returning heroes. Lucky bastards.

They eat.

So, why you been so quiet?

Bobby *shrugs.*

Rourke   Huh?

Bobby   Just.

Rourke   What?

Bobby   Just.

Rourke Just what?

Bobby Never knew what to say.

Rourke Jesus, kid, no one knows what to say, they just say it. I mean, listen to those goons today. They just open their mouths and shit falls out. They don't make sense half the time.

Bobby My mum says, 'Say less, learn more.'

Rourke Yeah? Clever lady. So what have you learned so far?

Bobby Are you a gangster, Mr Rourke?

Pause.

Rourke Now that you're talkin' to me you might as well call me Johnny.

Bobby Are you a gangster?

Rourke What do you think?

Pause.

Bobby The other men. They do what you tell them to do?

Rourke Yeah. I'm kind a' second-in-command, I suppose. Kind a' like Mr Spock. My dad and Mr Sullivan were good friends. Dad died and . . . well, he looked out for me.

Bobby Who looked out for him?

Rourke Harvey Marr. Brooklyn legend. Decorated war hero. Last of his kind. Did for Sullivan what Sullivan did for me.

Bobby Is he a good man?

Rourke Your uncle? If it wasn't for him I'd probably be dead in a gutter with a knife in my guts years ago. He taught me somethin'. 'Self-worth' he calls it. He's as good as you get. True to his word. My word is iron.

Bobby He said that.

Rourke And he means it. He means it.

They eat in silence. Then . . .

Bobby   I'm sorry about your shoes.

Rourke   Don't mention it, kid.

They continue to eat in silence as the lights fade on them.

Blackout.

Scene Four

Sullivan's *place.*

A phone rings in darkness, then finally is silent.

Lights slowly up on **Sullivan** *and* **Rourke**. **Sullivan** *sits behind his desk, a black Bakelite phone to his right.* **Rourke** *stands before the desk. The door behind* **Rourke** *is slightly ajar.*

Sullivan   Sit down.

Rourke   Bobby's outside.

Sullivan   Close the door.

Rourke   What about Bobby?

Sullivan   Close the door and sit.

Rourke *goes to the door, closes it and takes a seat in front of* **Sullivan**'s *desk.*

Rourke   Everything OK?

Sullivan   No. Everything is not OK.

Rourke   OK.

Pause.

Sullivan   Have you been drinking?

Rourke   What? No.

Sullivan   Look at me.

Rourke *looks at him.*

Rourke   We were at the diner. We had burgers, fries and Cokes.

Sullivan   Don't take him into bars.

Rourke   I didn't.

Sullivan   He's too young.

Rourke   I wouldn't.

Sullivan   His father was a drunk. I don't want Bobby to follow him.

Rourke   We were at the diner.

Sullivan   Is he alone out there?

Rourke   Yeah.

Sullivan   Bring him in.

Rourke   You want him to hear this?

Sullivan   He might learn something.

Rourke   You sure?

Beat.

Rourke *goes to the door and beckons.* **Bobby** *enters. He seems to stand taller than before.*

Sullivan   Hello, Bobby. Why don't you wait by the door? Myself and Mr Rourke are going to have a business conversation. You're welcome to listen in.

Bobby *sits and* **Sullivan** *returns his full attention to* **Rourke**.

Sullivan   I received a phone call.

Rourke   From who?

Sullivan   Marconi.

Rourke   What did he want?

Sullivan   Well, he wasn't calling for a chat.

Rourke   Was it about the money?

Sullivan *nods.*

Rourke   Well, what did he say?

Sullivan   He said he sent it.

Rourke   When?

Sullivan   He said that he sent it over yesterday.

Beat.

He was phoning to inquire if I had received it and why I hadn't contacted him.

Rourke   You didn't get it?

Sullivan   No, I didn't.

Rourke   Shit.

Sullivan   Indeed. It gets worse.

Pause.

He said the two men who were delivering the money have gone missing.

Rourke *laughs nervously.*

Rourke   Well, that's convenient.

Sullivan   How is it?

Rourke   He's lying.

Sullivan   He gave me his word.

Rourke   And you believe him?

Sullivan   His word of honour.

Rourke   And what's that worth?

Beat.

Sullivan   It was his two most trusted men: Manfreedi and Mickey No-No.

Rourke   So they ran.

Sullivan   Unlikely.

Rourke   Yeah. Maybe they were pissed at him or somethin'. They take the money and run.

Sullivan   For a hundred grand? I don't think so. Two connected men don't disappear indefinitely for that kind of money. It's diminutive. A million maybe. No. They didn't run.

Pause.

Rourke   Alright. So, assuming Marconi sent the money with these goons and assuming they didn't run off with it, where does that leave us?

Sullivan   I told Marconi, if there was foul play whoever was responsible would pay with their life. I swore to him. I gave him an oath.

He studies **Rourke** *in silence.*

Sullivan   Did you mention our conversation yesterday to anyone?

Rourke   What? No.

Sullivan   You're sure?

Rourke   I told the boys about the truce with Marconi, like you said, but I never mentioned the money.

Sullivan   You're sure, John?

Rourke   I swear on my life.

Pause.

Sullivan   What's your opinion of O'Hare?

Rourke   Mary? Honestly?

Beat.

Rourke   He's an asshole.

Sullivan   Why?

Rourke   He's dumb as shit.

Sullivan   Appearances can be deceptive.

Rourke   You think he plays dumb?

Sullivan   Maybe.

Rourke   He's too stupid for that.

Sullivan   He is Chief of Police.

Rourke   So he's good at kissin' ass.

Beat.

Sullivan   Do you trust him?

Rourke   I dunno, Mr Sullivan.

Sullivan   Should I trust him?

Rourke   You once told me to trust no one. Except family.

Sullivan *nods gravely.*

Sullivan   Just keep him at a distance. Be wary of him. Be casual, but be wary.

Rourke   OK.

Sullivan   In the meantime, it's in our interests as well as Marconi's to find these two men. If they can be found, I want the truth from them. They were driving a white Buick Riviera.

Sullivan *pushes a piece of paper towards* **Rourke**, *who picks it up.*

Sullivan   That's the registration number. We're not doing this through the cops, so find other means. Put O'Keefe on to it. Ryan back from Chicago? Send him out too. If they are out there and breathing I want to be the first to talk to them. Understand?

Rourke *nods.*

Sullivan   Watch your back.

Rourke *leaves.*

Sullivan   Bobby, I need you to keep a low profile for a while, OK? No going out by yourself, even to the corner store.

Pause.

Bobby   Uncle Sullivan?

Sullivan   Bobby?

Bobby   I don't like him.

Sullivan   Who?

Bobby   The man you were just talking about. The policeman. I don't trust him.

Sullivan   Why do you say that?

Bobby   I don't like the way he looks at you.

The lights slowly fade.

Music: 'Born on the Bayou' by Creedence Clearwater Revival.

Blackout.

Act Three

Scene One

The Shamrock bar.

Lights up slow stage right on a man strapped to a wheeled swivel chair, head slumped, unconscious. He has his back to us. Around him the floor is splashed with drying blood.

Several feet away, opposite and facing the anonymous man in the chair, **Lumpy Flannegan** *kneels, slumped and motionless as if asleep or deep in prayer. A half-eaten hotdog lies on the ground beside him.*

The lights slowly reveal **Wicklow** *and* **Antrim**, *who stand stage left at the jukebox. They drink bottles of beer and share a joint. Casual.*

Wicklow Thirty years he gets. For choppin' up his wife. They put him in for life but he's out in thirty years. They put him in Penn State. He comes out a fuckin' automaton. Know what that is? A robot. Nothin' in his eyes. Dead inside. How he got his name: Sorrow. Empty. Looks like he just shat a cat. Now, to prepare him for the world outside of his incarceration they teach him a trade. A good idea. Huh? Except that they teach him butchery. OK? They teach a guy who chopped up his wife into tiny little fuckin' pieces how to use a machete properly. Go figure. So what have we got? So now the guy's an artist. Best butcher in the city. But no one will employ him. On account of his homicidal tendencies. One night he's sittin' here drunk at the bar contemplatin' all manner of suicide and who, who should walk in?

Antrim Who?

Wicklow Harvey Marr. Drunk as funk. Bingo-bango. The rest, my friend, is history. Sullivan's got himself a professional waste-disposal unit. Practically provided and paid for by the government. So, you see? The law? It's a joke. Doesn't work. The justice system? Fuck it.

Antrim Yeah.

Wicklow   Tell me about it.

Antrim   What's the matter with him, anyways?

Wicklow   I just told yous.

Antrim   No. Harvey. He's crazy, right?

Wicklow   He drinks too much. Legendary. Back in the day, on the streets they called him Drum Belly.

Antrim   Why's that?

Wicklow   Used to take punches in his stomach for drink. A real iron man.

Antrim   Jeez.

Wicklow   Did a lotta drugs. Got one of his nuts shot off in the war.

Antrim   Guy's crazy.

Wicklow   His left one.

Antrim   A postman?

Wicklow   Go figure.

Antrim   I like 'im an' all, but he's nuts. Postmen are people.

Wicklow   He asks you to go for a drink with him, don't.

Antrim   Why?

Wicklow   Don't oblige him.

Antrim   Why?

Wicklow   You'll regret it.

Antrim   Why?

Wicklow   He asks me. Two beers in, he shoots a guy.

Antrim   Who?

Wicklow   Huh?

Antrim   Who was the guy?

Wicklow   I dunno. Neither does he. He's just some guy. He shoots him in the knee and shits in his car.

Antrim   No.

Wicklow   Yes.

Antrim   The guy's car?

Wicklow   Yes. The driver's side.

Antrim   Fuck.

Wicklow   Exactly. He must a' been drinkin' beforehand.

Rourke *enters with* **Bobby** *in tow.* **Rourke** *instantly sees the man in the chair and freezes.*

Antrim   Hiya, boys.

Rourke   What is this?

Wicklow   What?

Rourke   Bobby, go wait in the car.

Bobby   I wanna stay.

Rourke   Bobby –

Bobby   I'm staying.

Rourke   What in the name of Christ is happening here?

Wicklow   What?

Rourke   What am I seeing?

Wicklow (*indicates the victim*)   This? Sullivan's orders.

Rourke   He ordered this?

Wicklow   Yeah.

Rourke   Bullshit. Bobby wait in the car.

Antrim   Let 'im stay. Kid's seen worse.

Rourke (*to* **Antrim**)   Shut up. (*To* **Wicklow**.) Sullivan ordered this?

Wicklow   Yeah.

Rourke   He told you to do this, in person?

Wicklow   Yeah. What's the problem?

Rourke   What's the problem? The problem? Lemme see. What's the problem? (*He points at the man in the chair.*) He's the Chief of fuckin' Police!!

Wicklow *stares at* **Rourke** *blankly.*

Wicklow   So?

Rourke   You don't see a problem?

Wicklow   He's an asshole. Even you said.

Rourke   Christ!

Wicklow   What?

Rourke *quickly gathers himself.*

Rourke   Is he dead?

Antrim   Not yet.

Rourke   This is fucked- up.

Wicklow   You wanna beer?

Rourke   Why did Sullivan order this?

Wicklow   Didn't say.

Rourke   Well, what did he fuckin' say?!

Wicklow   Hey, don't get grumpy.

Rourke   Tell me, William.

Wicklow   He said invite the Chief round for drinks in the bar today. Lock the doors, rough him up and ask him what he knows about the money.

Rourke   The money?

Wicklow   Yeah. The money.

Rourke   What money?

Wicklow   He didn't specify. He just said to ask him what he knows about the money.

Rourke (*to himself*)   What the fuck would he know about the money?

Wicklow   What money?

Rourke   What?

Wicklow   You know somethin' we don't?

Rourke   Jesus.

Wicklow   Huh?

Rourke   Bobby. *Over here.*

Wicklow   Huh?

Rourke   He say anything?

Wicklow   Huh?

Antrim   Has this got somethin' to do with the Italians?

Wicklow   Shut up.

Rourke   What did he say?

Wicklow   Who?

Rourke   The man you have tied to the chair, fuckwit!

Wicklow   Don't use that tone with me, Johnny. I'm getting tired of it.

Rourke   Yeah? Oh, I'm sorry. Fuck you! You're an idiot. Both of ya. Do you know what you have done here?

Wicklow   Mr Sullivan's orders.

Rourke   Can't believe this. He tell you to stick a gun up your ass and pull the trigger, you do that too?

Antrim   Ours is not to question why, Joh –

Rourke   Shut up. (*To* **Wicklow**.) What did he say, O'Hare?

Wicklow   Oh, he said plenty.

Antrim   He's got a real dirty mouth on him. The language /
you could a' toasted marshmallows with.

Rourke   Did he fess up?

Wicklow   Denied all knowledge of any money but what
Sullivan gave him in an envelope yesterday. Know how much
he got? Two grand. When am I gonna see that kinda money?
I do more for Mr Sullivan than that tub of horseshit. I got
bills. I got pressing matters. I gotta a cousin needs a . . . an
operation or somethin'.

Rourke (*to* **Lumpy**)   Get up, Tommy.

Lumpy *doesn't move.*

Rourke   Lumpy!

Rourke *looks at* **Wicklow** *and* **Antrim**.

Rourke   What's the matter with him?

Antrim *starts to giggle uncontrollably.*

Rourke   Are you high?

Wicklow *laughs and tries to keep a straight face.*

Rourke   What?

Wicklow   Lumpy's dead.

Rourke   *What?*

Antrim   Dead. Definition: deceased. Synonyms . . .

Wicklow *and* **Antrim** *laugh.*

Rourke   What happened?

Antrim   Funniest thing you ever seen.

Rourke   What – Bobby, get away from him. What happened?

Wicklow   It was his turn to hit on the Chief.

Antrim   The funniest thing.

Wicklow   So he goes at it like a maniac. We'd been winding him up a little an' all, callin' him Fatty and what not, so he nearly takes the Chief's head off. 'How'd ya like them apples, Mary?!' Boom! He's screamin': 'How'd ya like them apples?!' Then he stops, an' I thought he must a' bust his wrist or somethin' 'cause he grabs his arm and makes this little . . .

Wicklow *and* **Antrim** *laugh.*

Wicklow   This little squeak noise –

Antrim   Like a little fat mouse –

Wicklow   Then down he goes. Like a cow in a slaughterhouse. Lights out. I gotta say it was amusing.

Antrim   Look on his face like he just shit himself.

Wicklow   Squeak. Down he goes.

Antrim   Fuckin' priceless.

Rourke   Poor bastard.

Antrim   Like Harvey would say, 'Waste of space.' Him and Sorrow got a busy night.

Rourke   This is nuts.

Wicklow   Two grand.

Rourke   Look at ya. How could you be so stupid? How? Laurel and fuckin' Hardy.

Wicklow   Hey!

Rourke (*to* **Bobby**)   You see this?

Wicklow   Hey.

Rourke *indicates the room, the world.*

Rourke   You see this, kid?

Wicklow   I don't like your tone.

Rourke   Welcome to fuckin' Brooklyn, Bobby.

Wicklow   I don't like your tone no mores. Never did.

Rourke   Idiots.

Wicklow   I don't have to be talked to like that. I'm not gonna be talked to like that. We won't take that, will we, Danny?

Antrim *shrugs.*

Wicklow   We won't be talked to like that.

Rourke   Don't you see what you've done? This is it. You can't just sweep this under the carpet. This is serious. This is the goddam it. You hear me? This is the worst. This is FBI. We're dead men. All of us. This is it.

Wicklow   What is?

Rourke   Use your fuckin' brain, the two of ya. Jesus mother.

Wicklow   So what are you sayin'? We're in trouble?

Rourke   You have no idea.

Wicklow   It was Mr Sullivan's orders.

Rourke   Shut up. I'm thinkin'.

Wicklow (*quietly*)   His say-so.

O'Hare *groans and stirs. They all look at him.*

Rourke   Shit.

O'Hare   Motherfuckers.

Rourke   Hello, Mary.

O'Hare   Son of a bitch.

Rourke   There seems to have been a . . . little misunderstanding.

O'Hare *spits blood.*

Rourke   I don't suppose if we let you go you'd forget all about this?

O'Hare   You're dead men.

Rourke   I'm inclined to agree with you.

O'Hare   Assholes, the lot a' ya. Bunch of ignorant micks.

Rourke   Jesus.

O'Hare   You are in so much trouble it's unbelievable. You hear me?

Rourke   I need a drink.

O'Hare   Immigrant fucking MICKS!!

Wicklow   Hey! Pot, kettle, fuckin' black!

O'Hare   Bastards.

Rourke   Shut up! (*To the others.*) Look at me.

Wicklow, **Bobby** *and* **Antrim** *look at* **Rourke**.

Rourke   Ignore him.

O'Hare   Bog-hoppin', muck-savage Irish bastards.

Rourke   Whatever he says. Just . . .

He goes to fix himself a whiskey and ice.

O'Hare   You're all goin' down for this. You're dead men. You hear?

Rourke   Bob, you wanna Coke? Bobby?

O'Hare *lifts his head and his gaze finds* **Bobby**.

O'Hare   Hello, Bobby boy.

He stares up at **Bobby** *with a busted smile.*

O'Hare   You tell that uncle of yours . . . You tell that son of a bitch I'll see him in hell.

Rourke   Shut up.

O'Hare (*to* **Bobby**)   You hear that, you little cocksucker?

Bobby *takes a step towards* **O'Hare**.

Rourke   Bob.

O'Hare   You tell him from me he's fuckin' extinct.

Rourke   Shut up.

O'Hare (*to* **Bobby**)   You too, kid.

Rourke   Bobby, get over here.

O'Hare   You're dead meat, you little Irish shit, you all are.

Rourke (*to* **O'Hare**)   You shut up. I'll make you suffer, I swear.

O'Hare   You're nothin'.

Rourke (*to* **Wicklow** *and* **Antrim**)   One of yees stick a sock in his mouth.

O'Hare   You're dirt!

Rourke   Shut up!

O'Hare   Ditch-digging dirt!

Rourke   Shut the fuck up!

O'Hare   Potato-eatin' white niggers!

Bobby *strides purposefully over to* **O'Hare** *and thrusts something deep into his sternum, puncturing the heart. As* **O'Hare** *thrashes briefly against his binds,* **Bobby** *stabs him savagely and repeatedly in the chest. Only when* **O'Hare** *is still does* **Bobby** *stop. The boy drops something metallic and bloody to the floor. The others stare at him in dumbfounded silence.* **Bobby** *uses his left hand to wipe a drop of blood from his cheek. Then with his bloodied right hand he repeats this action, covering his face with blood.*

Rourke   Christ, Bobby.

Bobby   He shouldn't have said those things.

Rourke   Jesus.

He goes to **Bobby**. *Uses a handkerchief to pick the metal object from the floor.*

Rourke Where'd you get this?

Bobby My mum.

Rourke A knife?

Bobby A letter-opener. For opening her letters.

Rourke *wipes the blood from the weapon.*

Rourke What does this read?

Bobby 'Titanic'.

Rourke It says 'Titanic' on it.

Bobby You know? The big ship that sank.

Silence.

Antrim You know what the ironic thing is?

Rourke *looks at* **Antrim,** *a murderous look.*

Blackout.

Scene Two

Sullivan's place.

Sullivan *is seated behind his desk.* **Rourke** *paces around the room like a hunted animal.*

Rourke . . . And you know what the *ironic* thing is? You wanna know what the ironic thing is? O'Hare's father *drowned* on the *Titanic*. What are the odds? Huh? What are the fucking odds!?

Sullivan Johnny –

Rourke I'm a nervous fuckin' wreck. You're pullin' the world out from underneath me. I don't know what's up and what's down any more. Jesus. I don't know what's back and forwards. Who's who? What's what? What the hell were you thinking?

Sullivan   Simmer down, Johnny.

Rourke   What the hell were you *thinking*, Gulliver?

Sullivan   It was necessary.

Rourke   Necessa – What have you done?

Sullivan   What had to be done.

Rourke   Jesus . . .

Sullivan   He couldn't be trusted.

Rourke   I feel sick.

Sullivan   You're part of the wheel that's spinning, Johnny.

Rourke   What does that mean?

Sullivan   You're spinning.

Rourke *looks at* **Sullivan** *with a danger in him.*

Rourke   I never thought I'd say this. But I doubt you.

Sullivan   It's only fools don't question. Allow me to explain. Relax. You breathing again? Good. Now, listen to me. I have reason to believe that Chief O'Hare intercepted the money.

Rourke   'Reason to believe'?

Sullivan   I have my sources.

Rourke   Who?

Sullivan   That's on a need-to-know basis.

Rourke   Well, I need to know.

Sullivan   No, you don't.

Rourke   Then what am I?

Sullivan *looks at him, unreadable.*

Rourke   What am I? Huh? Just a lackey? Is that what I am to you? Another one of your goons? Your footsoldiers? Am I like Wicklow? Like Danny fuckin' Antrim? You told me I was your left hand.

Sullivan *looks at him, unreadable still.*

Rourke   You told me you trusted me.

Sullivan   Johnny, your father was a good friend.

Rourke   Then why don't you talk to me before you take these leaps?

Sullivan   Leaps?

Rourke   This. These. These giant leaps. These fuckin' . . . these rash decisions?

Sullivan   I think. I decide. I do. And I've been doing this since before you were born.

Pause.

Sullivan   No one will come looking for us. O'Hare will be buried under Hennessey's floorboards. It's public knowledge they didn't like one another. Hennessey killed O'Hare and chose to disappear. Tomorrow the cops get an anonymous tip-off. It's all sewed up. Watertight.

Beat.

Rourke   What about Bobby?

Sullivan   What about him?

Rourke   He killed a man today.

Sullivan   His father did the same thing at his age and he didn't turn out so bad.

Rourke   You said he was a drunk.

Sullivan   He was. He cleaned himself up.

Rourke   Then why's the kid so screwed-up? What's he doin' over here?

Sullivan   Bobby has seen worse than Hennessey's death.

Pause.

Yes. He told me. He's blood.

Beat.

He's got a warrior's heart. The trouble he was involved in. He came home to find his father beating his mother. He knocked him unconscious with a firearm and kicked him to death.

Rourke   His own father?

Sullivan   Stepfather. His real father didn't know he existed until a couple of weeks ago.

Pause.

Rourke   You?

Sullivan   I only knew his mother one night. I'm not proud of that. But now maybe I can make amends.

Rourke   Jesus.

Sullivan   Bobby doesn't know any of this yet.

Rourke   Jesus.

Sullivan   When the time is right.

Rourke   He's a killer.

Beat.

He's a killer, Gulliver.

Sullivan   Natural born.

Rourke   He's your son.

Sullivan   Like I said. I haven't turned out so bad. Have I?

They look at one another.

An uneasy silence.

*The telephone on **Sullivan**'s desk rings loudly. **Sullivan** doesn't move. **Rourke** finally looks at the phone, then at **Sullivan**.*

Sullivan *smiles and motions vaguely towards the phone.* **Rourke** *reaches for the receiver and picks it up.*

Rourke   Rourke . . .

He listens for a few moments then hangs up.

Rourke   O'Keefe and Ryan found the car.

Sullivan   The money?

Rourke *shakes his head.*

Sullivan   The two men?

Rourke   They got one of them. Mickey No-No.

Blackout.

Scene Three

The Shamrock bar.

Lights up on the bar. A dark slick of blood in the middle of the floor. O'Hare's blood. A dishevelled-looking man in a crumpled white suit sits unbound on the swivel chair where we found O'Hare earlier. His head shakes briefly for a moment then stops. A nervous disorder. This is **Mickey No-No**.

The bodies of **Lumpy** *and* **O'Hare** *lie off to the side in shadow.*

Wicklow *leans by the door watching* **No-No**.

Wicklow   Wop.

Pause.

Hey, rubber neck.

No-No *glances nervously at* **Wicklow**.

Wicklow   Fuck you lookin' at?

Pause.

The sound of footsteps. The door opens and **Sullivan** *enters followed by* **Rourke** *and* **Bobby**. **Sullivan** *removes his coat and hands it to* **Wicklow**.

Sullivan   He say anything?

Wicklow   Nothin'. Every now and then he shakes like he's on spin.

Sullivan   You been nice to him?

Wicklow   Oh yeah. Real hospitable. They found this fuck under a sewer bridge in New Jersey.

Sullivan   Watch your language William, we have a minor present.

Wicklow   Sorry, kid.

Sullivan *walks over to* **No-No**. *He studies him for a moment in silence.* **No-No** *stares mutely at the pool of blood around his feet.*

Sullivan   Hello, Michael.

No-No *continues to stare at the blood.*

Sullivan   You hear that?

Silence.

That's your heartbeat.

Beat.

Bobby, come over here will you?

Bobby *walks over and stops by* **Sullivan***'s side.* **Bobby** *stares at the blood without looking at* **No-No**.

Sullivan *indicates* **No-No**.

Sullivan   Bobby, would you trust this man?

Bobby *and* **No-No** *look at each other briefly.* **Bobby** *nods his head.*

Sullivan (*to* **Bobby**)   Thank you. (*To* **Wicklow**.) William, why don't you take Bobby for an ice cream.

Wicklow   Sure thing.

Bobby *takes one last look at* **No-No** *then exits with* **Wicklow**.

Pause.

Sullivan *dips the tip of his shoe into the blood and begins the slow process of writing a word on the floor in O'Hare's blood. He speaks quietly and calmly as he does this.* **No-No**'s *head begins to shake.*

Sullivan   You know whose blood this is? I believe you were acquainted. Police Chief Marion O'Hare. You see, what happened was he ceased to be of use to me. In fact, the man ceased to have any usefulness to society whatsoever. All he did was take. Take, take, take. Never satisfied. Beware the man whose appetite is never sated. He'll eat you up. Every last bit. Yum-yum-bubble-gum. And then? Then he'll most probably devour himself. It's a terrible trait in the Irish. Hunger. We never forgot it. We were oppressed and denied for so long, now we feel entitled to everything, and more. Creatures of excess. One day it'll be our downfall.

Sullivan *has finished writing the word in blood. He steps back. He walks behind* **No-No** *and views his work.*

Sullivan   Can you read that? What does it say?

No-No (*quietly*)   'Honesty'.

Sullivan   I'm sorry? You're going to have to speak up.

No-No   'Honesty'.

Sullivan   That's right, Michael. It says 'Honesty'. It's the best policy.

He takes a chair and places it in front of **No-No**.

Sullivan   I'm on the brink of a war here, Michael. Very messy. Now. Clean it up. Answers. What I require from you is the truth. Plain and simple. Give me facts. Explain things as they happened. I ask a question, you answer it. It's very simple. Tell me the truth and as a reward I will allow you your life.

No-No*'s head shakes uncontrollably.*

Sullivan   But, I warn you, Michael. I'll know if you're lying. It's a knack I have. Do I make myself clear?

No-No *can't help but shake his head.*

Sullivan   Is that a yes or a no, No-No?

No-No   That's a yes, Mr Sullivan.

Sullivan   Good man. Then let's begin.

Sullivan *sits facing* **No-No**, *crosses his legs, leans back and smiles.*

Sullivan   How well did you know Chief O'Hare?

No-No   I just had a drink with him.

Sullivan   You drank with him?

No-No   Once. In Joe's Bar. Marconi introduced me.

Sullivan   Marconi introduced you to O'Hare?

No-No   Yes.

Sullivan *looks at* **Rourke***: 'I told you so.'*

Sullivan   What did you talk about?

No-No   I dunno. The moon? Everybody was talkin' about the moon.

Sullivan   Did O'Hare know about this delivery? The money. Was it mentioned?

No-No   I dunno.

Sullivan   Did O'Hare take my money?

No-No   No. I don't know.

Pause.

Sullivan   Where's my money, Michael?

No-No   I . . . I . . . I don't know.

Sullivan   Not a good start.

No-No   I don't know where it is, I swear.

Sullivan   Where's Manfreedi?

No-No   I dunno.

Sullivan   'I dunno. I dunno.' What do you know?

No-No   Nothin', I dunno nothin'.

Sullivan   That's not true, Michael. Everybody knows something.

No-No   I got kids . . .

Sullivan   Why did you run, No-No?

No-No   I panicked. Please, Mr Sullivan –

Sullivan   Ah-ah. Let's keep this professional. Why did you panic?

No-No   Manfreedi. He didn't come back.

Sullivan   Back? From where? Expound.

No-No   Huh?

Sullivan   He 'didn't come back'?

No-No   Yes. I mean, no. He didn't. I was driving, see? I'm in the driver's seat, waiting.

Sullivan   Where was this?

No-No   Couple a blocks from here.

Sullivan   When?

No-No   Yesterday. Before lunch.

Sullivan   Go on.

No-No   So I'm sittin' there, listening to the car radio and I'm waitin' on Manfreedi comin' back.

Sullivan   Manfreedi was delivering the money?

No-No   Yeah, the package. He's gone, I dunno, maybe a minute? And then . . .

He starts to shake.

Sullivan   It's alright, Michael. You're nervous. That's understandable. In your position I'd be terrified. Take a deep breath.

No-No *breathes deep.*

Sullivan   That's good. Take another one.

No-No *breathes again.*

Sullivan   Good.

Sullivan *breathes deep.*

Sullivan   Good. And another.

No-No *breathes again.*

Sullivan   It's all in the breath.

Sullivan *breathes again.* **No-No** *breathes again.*

Sullivan   There we go.

No-No   Thank you.

Sullivan   Don't thank me. Now. Manfreedi has the package.

No-No   Yes.

Sullivan   My money.

No-No   Yes.

Sullivan   He's gone a minute. And then?

No-No   He's gone maybe a minute and then, then I think I hear gunshots.

Sullivan   You think?

No-No   Radio's on. I'm singin' along to it.

Sullivan   What's the tune?

No-No   Huh?

Sullivan   What's the tune? What are you singing along to?

No-No   'Raindrops Keep Falling on My Head'.

Sullivan   That's a nice tune.

No-No   It is. It's the best day of my life. My wife . . .

He starts to weep. **Sullivan** *watches him.*

She gave gave birth to a baby boy yesterday. I got two daughters. It's my first boy.

Sullivan   Congratulations. You heard gunshots . . .

No-No *recovers.*

No-No   They just sounded like little pops.

Sullivan   How many?

No-No   I dunno.

Sullivan   How many?

No-No   Maybe two. Maybe three.

Sullivan   Then?

No-No   I turn off the radio. I listen but there's nothin'. I waited maybe one minute. Maybe two. Manfreedi didn't come back. That's when I panicked. I got outta there. I just drove around. I couldn't think straight. I was thinkin', 'How bad is this?' I'm thinkin' how bad is this gonna look for me, ya know? Maybe people thinkin' that I stole the goddam money, ya know? But I didn't. I swear on my mother's life. Manfreedi had the money. He didn't come back. I waited. But he was . . . he was *gone.* I just drove around. I couldn't see no sign of him. There weren't that many people around, ya know? I looked everywhere. Everywhere. I was lookin' everywhere for the colour of the uniform, but he was gone.

Sullivan   Uniform?

No-No   Yeah. It was Manfreedi's idea. He was paranoid the
FBI were watching him. They been all over Marconi, ya
know? So as not to draw attention, he made the delivery in
disguise, you know? His idea being, 'Who's gonna look twice at
a postman?'

Rourke   A postman?

No-No   Yeah. The money was in a postman's sack . . .

Silence.

Sullivan *stares at* **No-No**.

Rourke *slowly lowers his head.*

Sullivan *opens his mouth but no words come out. Subtly the man's
entire nature seems to change. It is like his whole being seems to quietly
exhale. He slowly pulls himself to his feet, takes a deep breath and then
suddenly, violently releases it in a terrifying howl of rage:*

Sullivan   YOU GOTTA BE FUCKING ME!!

Music: 'I Wanna be Your Dog' by The Stooges.

Blackout.

Epilogue

Darkness.

A church.

The lights slowly fade up to reveal **Harvey Marr** *sitting in a church pew in his pork-pie hat. He talks out, looking up at a crucified Jesus only he can see.*

Harvey You gotta help me out here. I'm at the end of it. You gotta answer me this question. I need to know. I been losing sleep over this. OK . . .

Beat.

Is it chimpanzees or gorillas eat their own shit?

Beat.

He explodes with laughter, a maniacal shuddering sound that quickly becomes ugly and desperate. The laughter swiftly subsides and becomes a kind of low moaning. The mouth smiles but the eyes betray a man who has given up the fight.

How was I to know he wasn't a postman? How? What is he doin' dressed as a postman? Who delivers a hundred grand in a mail sack? What was he thinkin'? What? How could I recognise him? He had a bullet in his face. Fuck deserves to be dead. Fuck 'im. Fuck me! I'm an idiot! You're an idiot, Harvey!

Pause.

I'm at the end here. You hear me?

Pause.

I said it.

Pause.

You want me to say it again?

I'm sorry.

Pause.

I'm sorry. Before Jesus and all his apostles, before you and all your heavenly angels . . . I'm sorry. I'm not askin' for my life. That's a given gone. I let down my pal. Only friend I ever had. I accept what's comin'. I embrace it. I intend to pay my dues. My life's worth nothin' anyways. I'm not askin' for that. I'm askin' for forgiveness. Blessed Virgin Mother Mary forgive me and deliver me up when the time comes. I see the error of my ways. I see 'em all. I see 'em laid out in front of me. I been a bad man. Yes. I'm not denying it. No. I lied and cheated and extorted and bullied and stole and killed. I killed more men than I care to remember. There's nothin' about the devil I don't know. But this is me. Here I am. This is me. Right here. Harvey Anthony Ignatius Marr. This is me. Offering up a prayer for the better of two eternities. I'm here. I ended up right here. I could a' been with a hooker or gettin' loaded in a bar, or gettin' loaded in a bar with a hooker, but I'm not. In my final hour I find myself standing here. I'm right here.

Pause.

I'm right here. Harvey 'Drum Belly' Marr. The Fightin' Irish. The end of an era. I'm right here.

Pause.

You want me to get down on my knees? Is that how it works? OK.

He gets down on to his knees. He takes off his hat and clasps it to his breast with both hands. He looks up at Jesus.

In the brightly lit church doorway upstage two figures silently appear in silhouette. **Sorrow** *and* **Rourke**.

Rourke *walks quietly forward and stops a respectful distance behind* **Harvey**, *who is unaware of him.*

Harvey   I'm listening. I want you to speak to me. Please. I'll hear you. I'm listening. I want you to say something. Say: 'I forgive you.'

He listens.

A long silence.

Then . . .

Rourke   Harvey.

Harvey *opens his eyes.*

Rourke   Time to go.

Pause.

Harvey   Walter with you?

Rourke   He's waiting outside.

Harvey *nods to himself.*

Harvey   Will you do me one last thing, Johnny? When you're done, send me home. The old turf. Even if it's just my heart. I wanna go home.

Rourke   Sure, Harve.

Harvey *crosses himself and stands.*

Harvey   They come back?

Rourke   Who?

Harvey   The moon men. They get back OK?

Rourke   Yeah. This mornin'.

Harvey   We're a miracle. That's the shame of it.

He looks up one last time.

Never said a word.

Rourke   Who?

Harvey   Not a word.

He places his hat back on his head, then walks upstage and disappears into the light.

Rourke *takes one brief look up at Jesus then follows him.*

Lights fade.

Music: 'Oh Happy Day' by the Edwin Hawkins Singers.

Blackout.